OCHO CINCO

OCHO

WHAT FOOTBALL AND LIFE

CINCO

HAVE THROWN MY WAY

CHAD OCHOCINCO
WITH JASON COLE

CROWN PUBLISHERS
NEW YORK

Copyright © 2009 by Chad Ochocinco

Published in the United States by Crown Publishers,
an imprint of the Crown Publishing Group, a division
of Random House, Inc., New York.

www.crownpublishing.com

CROWN and the Crown colophon are registered trademarks of
Random House, Inc.

Library of Congress Cataloging-in-Publication Data

Ochocinco, Chad, 1978–
Ocho Cinco / Chad Ochocinco. — 1st ed.
p.   cm.
1. Ochocinco, Chad, 1978–   2. Football players—United
States—Biography.   I. Title.
GV939.J6125A3 2009
796.332092—dc22
[B]

ISBN 978-0-307-46039-4

Printed in the United States of America

Design by Maria Elias

10 9 8 7 6 5 4 3 2 1

First Edition

CONTENTS

ONE

IF NOT THIS, WHAT WOULD I BE? 1

TWO

STUCK IN THE 'NATI 17

THREE

DON'T BLAME IT ON RAY 33

FOUR

COACHING OCHOCINCO 45

FIVE

GROWIN' UP 65

SIX

TALKING TRASH 83

SEVEN

WHY MY BEST GAME REALLY SUCKED 97

EIGHT

CELEBRATIONS 115

NINE

BELICHICK AND THE OTHER COACHES 133

TEN

OCHOCINCO, MARKETING GENIUS 147

ELEVEN

HOW DO YOU PLAY LIKE ME? YOU CAN'T 165

TWELVE
WOMEN 185

THIRTEEN
KING OF ALL SPORTS 199

FOURTEEN
WASTED DAYS AND WASTED NIGHTS 213

FIFTEEN
FAMILY AND FRIENDS 233

SIXTEEN
PLANET CHAD 245

People don't understand Chad. He's just trying to have fun playing. He's not hurting anybody. He's not embarrassing anybody, he's just playing. He's a kid and he's a really good dude. I love watching him and I know a thing or two about wide receivers. Is he one of these diva receivers that everybody talks about? Yeah, he is, but that's what we do, man. We're out there making the highlight plays. The plays that change the game, man. What do you expect us to be?

—**Michael Irvin,** Pro Football Hall of Famer and three-time Super Bowl champion wide receiver with the Dallas Cowboys

ONE

IF NOT THIS, WHAT WOULD I BE?

MY LIFE IS GOOD. It's sweet, so sweet. Roll up to my place in Plantation, Florida, and that's easy to see. Right there in the circular driveway that wraps around the fountain in my front yard you get the first taste.

Wait a second, I gotta let you in the front gate first. It's a gated community and all. But once you're in and riding by my huge-ass house on an acre of land, you can see what I'm saying. Parked in front are seven sweet-ass cars. One for every day of the week. I don't like to get bored, you know?

There's the Rolls-Royce for chillin'. There's the Hummer. The Dodge 4 × 4 Ram pickup. Nice dubs on that. Then there's the 1971 drop-top Caprice with the rims, the nice paint job, and an interior better than the day they brought it off the assembly line. Same goes for the 1973 Impala. That's a convertible, too. Hey, man, this is Florida.

Then there's the convertible Lamborghini. It's kind of a Cincinnati

Bengals orange. Man, who says I don't believe in the team? Finally, there's the Mercedes SLR McLaren. Mercedes makes 500 of those a year and it goes for a cool $500,000. That baby goes 0 to 60 in 3.6 seconds, which is only slightly quicker than me, and hits 208 mph, which is only a little faster than me.

Then again, most cornerbacks think I'm faster than that.

Come on in the crib. Don't get freaked out by the Plexiglas walkway over the koi pond with the little waterfall next to it, it'll hold you. The big room in the front with the marble tiles is cool and the upstairs room with the pool table is very cool. But the best room is the entertainment room just off the kitchen. In there are the three big-screen TVs. Yeah, three. That's not the best part, though. The best part is that the TVs are inset into a floor-to-ceiling aquarium that runs about 30 feet down one wall.

I got some beautiful fish in there, even a little baby shark. The TVs are built into the front of the aquarium, the wires coming down through some fake coral beneath each of the boxes. It's an awesome view.

I've got paintings of myself around the house. Back in my condo in Cincinnati, I've got like nine paintings of myself. Why? I love me some me, that's why.

And man, I love my things, especially my car. I got a 2008 Dodge Charger back in Cincinnati, painted up a little like the General Lee from *Dukes of Hazzard*. I don't have the orange. It's black and charcoal. But that car smokes, man. Just blazes. I got the '01 on the side, just like in the show. Only difference is that it says General Ocho Cinco on top, not General Lee. Hey, there's only so far you can take that whole idea.

I'm not getting into that whole Confederate flag shit and all. I am a black man, you know.

Now, I didn't like school at all. Hated it. Yeah, I'm smart and I could have done the work, but I didn't want people to know how smart I was and I couldn't sit there in all those stupid classes listening to all that boring stuff. No way. Football was my way out. I had to make it. Not that I did it the easy way. But I had to make it.

And if I hadn't made it in football, I would have done what I had to do. Whatever I had to do to get the things I like. At this point for me to have the nice things that I like, I wasn't good in school so that's down the drain. Therefore, I would have to resort to means of illegal activity to get the things that I like.

Yeah, if that means sell drugs, I would have done that. I'm not into drugs. Don't even drink. I go to the bar at J. Alexander's in Cincinnati and order drinks for everybody there. But I drink cranberry juice. That's it. But in my 'hood, to get the things that I wanted, that meant selling drugs, and back then I would have done that.

It's like what Pittsburgh wide receiver Santonio Holmes was talking about before the Super Bowl. By the way, sweet catch on the game-winner. Damn, how I wish I could get that chance to make that play. How sweet would that be?

Anyway, back to my point. Sometimes there aren't a lot of choices to get what you want. You have two ways out in life. You can make it as an athlete or you have to hustle. I give Santonio a lot of credit for being honest about what he was facing. We both grew up in South Florida, although I'm from Miami and he's from Belle Glade, which is more the country, sugarcane fields and all that. He talked to the *Miami Herald* about it one day and then shared even more in another interview the next day. Here's what Holmes said:

"I feel it's time to share things. I'm on the biggest stage. Everybody's going to be watching. I'm pretty sure some kids can get a feel for changing their lives and not doing those type of things, and can get an opportunity to get out of the ghetto, the 'hood, to be successful. My friends were always doing it and I felt comfortable doing it at the time. As the years grew older, I just felt like that wasn't what I wanted to do. I wanted to play football. I don't want to end up like a lot of my friends, in jail, standing on the corner, not going to school."

Some people thought Santonio shouldn't have said that stuff before the Super Bowl. But he was being honest, being real, talking about his life and what drives him to be great. I'm telling you the same things about me, what makes me want to be the best. What drives me and, really, what I would have been.

People think drug dealers are stupid, but they're not. Now, the ones who get caught, yeah, they're stupid. I wouldn't get caught.

How else would I get these things? Become some entertainer, a dancer? Yeah, I love music. I even play some instruments. Sax, guitar, piano a little. But that's not what I am. If you're going to be an entertainer, it starts when you are young, when you are four years old. You don't start when "Oh damn, football didn't work out for me, let me try this." It doesn't work that way. All actors start when they are young.

I hang out with musicians. During the bye week last year, I hung out with Lil' Wayne in his studio in Miami. That dude works hard. It was Saturday, like 1 A.M., when I showed up at his place and he's totally focused, totally into what he's doing. No breaks, not much conversation, he's just going and going, doing his thing. It was amazing to watch, but to think I could just cross over at a late age and really do that and be great at it, come on now.

That's why I tell you it was football or it was the street for me. Now, I'm not into the street life. NFL Security doesn't need to be bothering me. I know some guys who do that stuff from the old neighborhood where I grew up, Liberty City in Miami. I talk to those guys, but I don't live the street life and I don't want to. My grandma brought me up not to deal with that. I was either playing football or I was home. I didn't get in serious trouble. She was a teacher. She wouldn't have it.

Still, what I'm saying is that if football hadn't worked, I would have done illegal activities. I would have been Frank Lucas, the dude from *American Gangster*. That dude was real. As crazy as that shit sounded, he was real and he made it, big-time. This is what I'm saying about guys who survive in that business and really make it: They're smart. You know how Lucas burned the mink coat in the movie? Don't be flashy, don't show off what you have. Don't attract attention. That would have been me. You have to be smart to survive in that business. You're not trying to be some street guy who gets arrested all the time. That's stupid.

The ones who do the illegal stuff are bright. Some of them might be some of the smartest people in the world to get away and do some of the things they do. Not only do you have to be smart at what you do, you have to be able to outthink the system, outsmart the system. You have to watch over your shoulder 24/7. A lot goes into that. You don't know who's who.

5

Now, I'm sure the NFL doesn't like to hear that, but let's be real. Let's put it out there. This is what happened to me.

This is what this book is about. It's not just my story, it's me. It's about what I think, what I feel, why I do this. It's about what the NFL is, the side of the game you don't understand all the time. This is about what you don't hear or see about me because you really only see it through the perspective of the media, the people who wrap up my story in a few words or in some video and think, "Hey, this is what Chad Ochocinco is." That's just part of me.

It's like in 2008 at the Pro Bowl in Hawaii, when one reporter said that I "shoved" some guy [Michael Lipman] from the NFL who was trying to talk to me. I didn't shove him. The dude is like 5-foot-8. If I'd have shoved him, he'd have sued my ass. I pushed his hands away. Was I in a bad mood? Yeah, I was. I didn't want to talk to anybody, reporters, TV people, NFL PR guys, nobody. That's when I was on my big kick to try to get out of Cincinnati, which didn't work out so hot (more on that later).

Anyway, the dude from the NFL touched me and I pushed his hand away. That was it and then I left. But now everybody thinks I'm shoving guys to the ground, I'm fighting, committing assault and all sorts of crap that never happened. It was just typical BS that comes with being me. We got guys in other places doing crazy shit, like punching their quarterback in the face in the weight room, and it barely gets in the news.

You see, the funniest part is that people think I'm so bad, but do you see one arrest on me since I got to the NFL? Do you see me getting suspended for using drugs or steroids? Do you see anything about me beating up my girlfriend or some other guys? No, none of that. Still, people think I'm this bad guy because I do some celebrations and talk trash and I'm flamboyant. Look, I'm working hard, I'm having fun, and nobody is going to stop me from having fun.

Well, maybe the Bengals will, but that's another story for later. I'm not hurting anybody, but I push a guy's hand away and it's an international crisis. "Chad is flipping out in the Islands, what's going to happen? He might fly to Japan and start some shit there." They're making me out to be like Godzilla or something, stepping on buildings and knocking shit over. Yeah, that would be me, Chadzilla. Man, I ain't going to Japan. I don't even like sushi. Unless you got a sushi company you want me to endorse. I can see it now, try the Ochocinco sushi roll. It would be like a spicy tuna roll with tempura flakes. Damn, I'm getting hungry already.

Like I said, the NFL probably isn't going to want to hear some of what I have to say. The commish, Roger Goodell, is probably going to give me that look like, "Ocho, what did you do now?" But it's like I said before in that sign, you guys remember the one, "NFL, please don't fine me."

And this is why football was so important, why it was everything I did as a kid. It's why I love the NFL and I want to be the best part of the NFL. I'm that great player. When I wore the Hall of Fame jacket as a celebration, I didn't mean that disrespectfully. That's where I want to be. That's where I expect to be.

Even today, it's everything I am. Ask my boys from home. We'll be out at a club on Friday night before a game and I'll sometimes just be sitting there, daydreaming. I'm thinking about the game. I'm thinking about what I'm going to do. I'm zoned out on football, that's all. People can come up to me and say, "What up?" They look at me and think, that dude is in space. But that's where my head is at. It's all about football.

Ask my coaches, they'll tell you the same thing. Marvin Lewis, my head coach with the Bengals, he'll tell you. I call him at three or four in the morning sometimes, telling him, "I was thinking, we should run this play" or "We should do this." My head is always in the game. No matter what you think you see, no matter what you think the antics are about, I want to win. I know that football is first.

Most people out there will say, sarcastically, "Yeah right, Ocho, all you think about is football." They think I'm just about the celebrations, the dances, the marketing, that it's just about me. Look, the marketing is important. I want to be Ochocinco, the brand. Yeah, that's what I want. This is a business and I want the things.

But you know what I know? It's about winning. Nothing else matters unless you win. The year we made the playoffs was the best year of my career. That's what I play for. The day of that playoff game against Pittsburgh, the only playoff game we've had since I've been in Cincinnati, I was walking through the parking lot before the game, high-fiving people. I was geeked up. I was ready. People are offering me barbecue, chips, everything. It was so great. They're hyped, we're finally going to do something.

The atmosphere is awesome. It's what I wanted to do when I got to Cincinnati. Everybody said when I got there, "Oh, you don't want to be here, this team sucks." I told them, I want to be the guy who changes it for Cincinnati. I want to make the Bengals a champion. That's what I want. Because I know the winning has to come first. People don't give a shit about you unless you're winning. That's where you make a difference. That's how you get the things you really want.

Do you know what it would be like to be the player who brings championships to the Bengals? That would be amazing. It would be, "Man, do you see what these guys did to win a title?" That's why I wanted so bad to do that with the Bengals. You hear people in other sports say, "Oh, you have to be in a big market and win there to make it big." That's bullshit. This is the NFL. If you win championships, especially if you win them with a team that hasn't done anything before, that just makes you even bigger.

You saw what happened when St. Louis won a title in 1999? What did everybody call them? The Greatest Show on Turf. Torry Holt and Isaac Bruce were big-time. Kurt Warner went from some guy who was a bag boy to MVP. Marshall Faulk went from a nice running back to the best all-purpose runner in the league. Look at Baltimore, where they didn't even have a team for years, just like St. Louis. The Ravens win it and Ray Lewis is huge.

And the most obvious of all is Peyton Manning. He wins a title in Indianapolis. Indianapolis? That's not some big-ass market, you know what I'm saying? But if you turn on your TV, you can't go five minutes without seeing his face on some commercial. It's unreal and Peyton's pretty funny. That fake mustache commercial or the one where he holds back the chicken. That's funny.

I want to play for championships. Everything you get flows from winning. In this book, my coaches will tell you that. They know I want to win. I want the fuckin' ball because I believe I can help us win. That incident in the playoff game against Pittsburgh—and I'm going to say it again, that wasn't a fight. I'll explain it more later, but I didn't swing at anybody. Not my head coach [Marvin Lewis]. Not my receivers coach [Hue Jackson]. Nobody. That incident was about the fact that I got one pass in the first half of that game. One fuckin' catch in the first half and you're telling me we're trying to win this game.

Winning starts everything. Yeah, they'll come out and watch the games even if the team sucks (trust me, I know that). But the place is dead, people are leaving early, nobody is buying shit. I get it. That's why I want to win so bad. People think I just want to play because I'm into myself and that's it. They don't understand, I see the big picture.

I see what it takes to get the life I want. I see what it takes to escape the streets, to not have to sell drugs like so many of the people I grew up with in Miami. Like I said, I would have been right there with them, living that life. Thank God I don't have to worry about that stuff, because I am where I am. I have these things—these cars, this house, my kids, and my life—because of football. Because I work hard at football. Yeah, some people are jealous. They think I was just lucky to be born able to run, jump high, and catch. Whatever. There's lots of guys who can do all that. Just go back to the 'hood where I grew up, where lots of guys grew up. There's lots of guys who were great athletes back where I was from. It's just like when I say that there are a lot of guys from the 'hood who could do what Michael Phelps has done. I'm not saying what he did is easy. I'm saying there are a ton of guys who just don't have the focus or the surroundings to do that, but they have the physical ability.

That's why I say, "I'm Michael Phelps." I know that pissed a lot of people off that I would say that, thinking I was disrespecting what he did. I'm just saying that there are people who could do what he did. A lot of people. There's guys back in the 'hood who could do it if they put their mind to it. If they work at it.

That's why I say that I could beat anybody in any sport. I have the ability. I can do it. Lots of guys can do it. But you have to work hard. You have to want to do it and, for me, sometimes it takes a while to figure out what you have to do. If I knew then what I know now about school and how it held me back from getting what I wanted, I wouldn't have wasted my time the way I did. That was stupid. I cost myself at least a year in the pros because it took me three years to get through junior college. Three years! I'm serious. You're supposed to be done in two and I took three. Nobody wanted to touch me back then. No college. That's when I realized, I gotta get serious about this shit.

The only school that would touch me for one year was Oregon State and Coach Dennis Erickson. He didn't care, he just said come play up here, do your thing. So I did. I spent four months up there in Corvallis, Oregon. Nothing to do up there. I mean, nothing. I just played football and that was it. I think I went to class the first week and then I was done. Made sure I was there for attendance, whatever. I did enough to get myself to the Senior Bowl that year and that helped me get drafted. I should have been a first-round pick. That was ridiculous that I wasn't a first-rounder. But the reason was that teams couldn't trust me. You know what I'm saying? It was my fault that I didn't get drafted higher, because the teams couldn't trust me.

Even so, I've spent my entire career proving to them how wrong they were for not taking me. I can't be stopped in this game. Nobody can stop me. No cornerback can touch me. Shit, I don't even see cornerbacks. It's like they don't even exist when I'm out there. I talk to them just so I can keep them sharp, keep them on top of their game, because that keeps me going. That's why I talk so much trash. Never stop. Never let up. Even before the game, I'm talking to the guys on the other team.

You see, everybody works hard to get to the NFL, to get those things they want. You have to. I don't talk about how hard I work out or how much I run or how much I lift or how much film I watch. I don't want to hear about it and I don't want to talk about it, because that's what everybody does. You can't survive in this business if you don't work, you know what I'm saying? Yeah, maybe you're some freak of an athlete, like Lawrence Taylor or something, and you can make it for a while. But even when LT played, it was different. Guys didn't train year-round like they do now. We got all these minicamps and workouts and everything. We're basically training 11 months a year.

If you don't work, you're going to be gone. First, you're not going to survive the punishment. Can't do it, especially if you're one of them big dudes playing inside. You gotta be ready. Second, the coach ain't going to have it if you're not working out, if you're not ready. They're going to cut your ass in a heartbeat if you don't want to do it their way. No question about that.

That's why I say, don't tell me about working hard. I see all these players talking about how they run up and down hills, lift weights all day, do cardio 52 hours a day. Come on, you don't have a choice in this game. The choice you make is way back when, when you're growing up. That's where all those guys make the choice about whether they want to make it in sports or if they want to do something else.

Of course, there's been a lot of dudes to go through Cincinnati that have a ton of talent, but they have a hard time making it on the team, being successful. I'm not talking about Chris Henry. He's going to figure it out, man. He's good, he's super talented, no question. And he's learned. I really believe that. He saw that they ain't playin'. Commissioner Goodell, he's not playing anymore. All that shit that guys used to get away with, you can't do it. Most of the guys in the league, they're smart enough to figure it out. You don't have to be some genius to know that you have to follow the rules. Chris can figure that out. He's not going to mess it up again.

There are some guys who just can't do it. It's sad, really sad. Really talented guys, but their lives are so messed up, they can't handle it. I'll get into my own story later, but it's like Odell Thurman. He's a linebacker we had on the team. His whole family life was messed up. He was drinking, using drugs, and he was angry. He was fighting. He couldn't get it under control.

The worst part is he could play. He was a second-round pick in 2005. The dude had five interceptions his rookie year. I don't know anything about playing linebacker. All I can tell you is that if it's Ray Lewis at linebacker, he's good. But you know if a guy is a good athlete, and Odell Thurman was serious. A great athlete. Tough, he could run, come up and hit you in the mouth, chase you down. I heard he returned an interception 99 yards for a touchdown in college. I know it's college, but that's serious for a linebacker. He could be great. But he was the kind of dude who couldn't stay out of trouble. I know Marvin Lewis tried to get through to Odell. They tried again and again, but he couldn't do it.

By his second year, he got suspended by the league for four games. Then he got arrested and he was suspended for the whole season. He got suspended again in 2007 and again in 2008. The dude is a wreck, it's just really sad. That's a guy who doesn't have the skills to see the big picture. I'm not ripping him, I'm explaining what happens to so many guys, like the guys I grew up with who could have been great athletes. They could have been Michael Phelps. But they didn't have the skills to understand what they have to do.

For me, I have those skills. I'm one of those guys. That's why I have a sweet life.

The Bengals let Chad act like that for all those years. I mean, they made him the face of the franchise. They rewarded him for acting that way. I'm serious. And now they want to punish him for acting like that? I mean, come on, man, it's like how I raise my son. If I allow him to act out for all these years and then start punishing him for it when he gets to be 14 or 15, it's not going to make sense to him.

—**Willie Anderson,** former Cincinnati Bengals offensive lineman and four-time Pro Bowler

TWO

STUCK IN THE 'NATI

THE WAY I LOOK at the 2008 season is I made my bed, I had to sleep in it. Yeah, I wanted out of Cincinnati. I wanted to go to a winner. Dallas, Washington, wherever. Hell, I don't understand why they didn't trade me. They got offered two first-round picks for me. Well, OK, one of the picks was a conditional third-rounder that could have become a first-rounder. Look, I'm good. Hell, I'm great. I'm the best fuckin' receiver there's ever been. But a first- and a third- or maybe even two first-round picks! I don't understand how Mike Brown didn't take that.

He wouldn't. I went up there one time to meet with Mike. I like Mike. He's old-school, but he's cool. He understands. He knew what I wanted, but he just laid it out. "Chad, I'm not trading you, that's it." It wasn't a long discussion, because he just said what it was going to be. What am I supposed to say at that point? I mean, I said everything I could possibly say to that point. I went on every radio station, every TV station, every interview I could find and told them I wanted out.

I wore out ESPN. I made their job so easy, they didn't even have to worry about Brett Favre or Terrell Owens for like three months. I was so good to them, they made me editor of *ESPN The Magazine* for one issue. I mean, how sweet is that? I mean, finally they got some good ideas (just kidding, guys, I love you all).

Anyway, I got going in February at the Pro Bowl. I go on with Jim Rome after I hear that they're saying I was the problem in 2007, the big reason why we went 7–9 that season. Man, how stupid is that shit? Our fans would love to see 7–9 after what we did this season in 2008.

So I go on Rome and he's telling me that everybody thinks I'm arguing too much or that I cause problems or whatever shit they say. I say sarcastically, "I get the blame; the so-called best player. I'm the problem. Someone in-house is spreading this. Maybe they want me to quiet down and stop being me. That is not going to happen. I can't function that way. I tried it. It sucked. There was no excitement."

At this point, I'm already telling people like T. J. [Houshmandzadeh] that I'm not coming in, I'm totally playing this thing up. I gotta get people in Cincinnati freaked. Look, I know I'm pissing them off, but I figure this is the only way to get out. I gotta get Mike Brown thinking I'm crazy, that I'm too big a pain in the ass to deal with anymore.

Then, in March, on *ESPN First Take,* I made the hint about the trade even stronger. I said: "I want to continue my career wherever I have the opportunity to win a playoff game and get to the Super Bowl. That's where I want to be." Like, what else can I say? But I still get no reaction.

In April, I'm talking to ESPN again (it was like having my own PR agency, how great is this). You thought I made it clear before? This was like me spelling c-a-t for them. This was after Carson Palmer told the Cincinnati media that I would be there in the off-season and should be there.

"I want to make this very clear: I don't know where he got that. I made no assertion to Carson that I would do that. Nothing has changed from what I've been saying for three months that I don't want to play for the Bengals. . . . I want to be traded before the draft, and if that doesn't happen, I want to be traded as soon as possible. I don't intend on reporting to anything."

All the while, the Bengals aren't saying a thing, except Marvin Lewis telling reporters at the NFL owners' meetings in March that he's talked to me, the team isn't trading me, and that he wasn't talking about it again. All Marvin is telling me is that he's pissed at me. Not that it's going to last, but he hates all that crap. He wants everybody there in the off-season and he figures I'm messing up his plan. Oh well, I gotta do what I gotta do.

Like I said before, I was acting mad. I was acting crazy. I was putting on a show. I didn't show up in the off-season until I absolutely had to for the mandatory minicamp. Look, it wasn't all pretend, I was seriously upset that I was stuck there, but it was hard because in the back of my mind I wanted to be the guy to turn the team around, like I said. Hey, look, I'll do whatever I can to get traded, but I'm not costing myself a bunch of money. No way. I read my contract. I knew how far I could take it. I still played with some people in the media, telling them I wasn't sure I was going to go to the minicamp and stuff. I even told some of my teammates, like T. J. Houshmandzadeh and Carson Palmer, that I wasn't coming in. But I knew I had to be there. I know the story about Carl Pickens and how the Bengals tried to get their money back from him when he criticized the Bengals for keeping Bruce Coslett as head coach. Look, they can fine me a little bit here and there, but I'm not giving them back any serious cash.

I may be crazy. I'm not stupid.

So I show up for minicamp. The funny part is that I can't practice because I have bone spurs in my foot. I end up having to have surgery. I don't even practice, but we have all these meetings to discuss what's going to happen and how we're going to handle it, and I don't say a word. I think Mike Brown thought I was really going to flip the fuck out and do something crazy.

Look, I talk trash. Everybody knows that. Every once in a while, Mike sends a note down to me before we play in a big game or something and says, "Chad, keep it quiet this week, this is not a week to be talking." So, of course, that just makes me talk even more. What do you expect?

But after I got there for minicamp in Cincinnati in June, I realized this shit wasn't going to work with me getting what I wanted. Hey, I took it as far as I could, it's time to do what they want. So I didn't talk trash then and I didn't say a word all season. Not one, nothing. Just kept my mouth shut. I know that the Bengals were expecting me to explode at one point, but I wasn't going to do it. Like I say, I'm here to do my job.

WILLIE ANDERSON

former Cincinnati Bengals teammate now playing
for Baltimore

I love Chad, I really do. I make fun of him and I'll tell you right now, yeah, he can be a distraction. He can wig out sometimes. But that's what the Bengals wanted from him. I'm serious, that's what they wanted. They marketed Chad, allowed him to do all that stuff, let him go off and act all crazy, talking trash and celebrating.

I'm not into that nonsense, but you can't blame Chad. It's the team's fault for allowing that. They want it both ways with Chad. They want him to be this great player all the time who gets people to go to games. But then when things go bad, they don't want him to talk. They want him to fall in line like the rest of the guys on the team. You can't do that with Chad, there's no way. That's not what he's about. He's out there, having fun, talking trash, telling the world, "Hey, look at me." If you allow that on a football team, well, you reap what you sow.

Chad ain't a bad guy. He's not getting into fights with teammates or anything like that. I mean, you're kidding if you think Chad is going to hurt somebody. The problem with Chad is that you lose focus sometimes. It's hard work to win in this game even without all the nonsense. That's what the Bengals don't understand, not one little bit. They want to sell tickets, they don't want to win. They don't want to put in all the effort it takes to be good. I've seen that, just like Chad has. But now they're expecting Chad to be the guy to lead everybody, and they haven't taught him how to be a leader.

Like I said, it's like raising children. Like the way I raise my son. You want him to act a certain way in a certain situation, you have to teach him that. You have to teach him that certain stuff ain't OK to do. Yeah, kids are going to step out on you a little, try to figure it out on their own a little. You gotta do that. But when they go too far, you have to reel them back in and teach them.

The Bengals have never done that with Chad. Never.

What am I going to do? I've already let loose as much as possible, so what's the point of continuing to do it? It's just being a distraction, being an asshole. The world knows how I feel. It's a situation that I can't control. I made my opinion known and my opinion was somewhat true, whether you agree or disagree with it, or liked the way I handled it or not. I knew exactly what the hell I was talking about.

I came in and I didn't even think about the record. I don't think about none of that. I think about making sure I'm doing my part and I look like Chad Ochocinco on film whether we're losing or not.

And here's the thing: We went 4–11–1 in 2008 and I could see it coming. I could see that we were going to have a bad year. Like I said before, when I first got to Cincinnati, I wanted to be the answer. I wanted to be the solution, the guy that made Cincinnati great, turned everything around. I still want to be that guy, but after a while you realize you can't do it by yourself. You know some stuff is never going to change. So that's why I wanted out, why I wanted to go somewhere I could win.

This has nothing to do with Cincinnati or the people. It's all about the organization. I love Cincinnati. I really do. I love driving around, I love the condo I got there. I love sitting out there at this beautiful park near my place that overlooks the river. On the Fourth of July, they send this boat out on the river and have this huge fireworks show that's awesome. The city is great. I even like the cold, and I'm from Miami. Damn, that ought to be proof I really am crazy.

The people are great, too. I go to high school games sometimes and just see the people, the kids playing. I go hang with guys playing basketball at the gym near my place, rap with them about what's going on, and try to give them some advice. The people come up to me and greet me all the time, wish me well, don't hound me like crazy. The people in Cincinnati get it. They know what I'm about. I got nothing bad to say about the city or the people.

Heck, I can leave my car, the General Ocho Cinco, on the street, running to keep the heat on, and nobody bothers it. Nobody takes it. I'm serious. I do that sometimes if I'm only going to be a minute or two. People know it's my car. I mean, really, who's going to just drive off in a car that says "General Ocho Cinco" on top? I stop at the mall, go up to the CD shop, buy some music or some games, come back down, and the car is right there. It's all cool.

I go to my favorite breakfast place, the First Watch on Walnut Street, and nobody bothers me. Yeah, they look sometimes or somebody will pay for my breakfast or whatever. That's cool, and I appreciate it. But it's not like they're on top of me, bugging out about me, making me uncomfortable. I have nothing but love for the people in Cincinnati. I've got people I hang out with who I met my first day there after I got drafted. They helped me out and we're still tight to this day. They come over to my house, play video games, go out for dinner all the time. It's all cool.

The problem is the team. I'm not talking about the guys or the coaches. Everybody is trying. But it's like I said, you can see stuff coming. You know things are going to be bad at a certain point. I could see it months before last year. We struggled in 2007 and what did we do in the off-season? Nothing. We just lost more players, lost whatever fighting spirit a lot of these guys have.

It's been this way for a long time, it just took a while for it to really kick in for me, for me to understand it. My first couple of years in Cincinnati, we had Dick LeBeau as our head coach. LeBeau was cool. Really cool. LeBeau might be black in the wrong body. He would never scream, never say something like, "What the fuck?" Nothing ever got to him, he was like Dennis Erickson that way. That's why, even though he didn't win for us, he has been awesome in his career. He just helped Pittsburgh win another Super Bowl. The dude was like the father of the 3-4 defense. It sucked that they fired LeBeau, because it wasn't his fault. We were trying to get our shit together, but we were going through quarterbacks, guys like Akili Smith and Jon Kitna, trying to get that settled. That was before Carson Palmer came in. So this shit wasn't LeBeau's fault. I just remember the media came down real hard on LeBeau about how he should be fired. When they fired him, I just came in like in tears, saying, "We're good, we don't have to get rid of nobody, we're going to be all right." I remember that. I remember how LeBeau used to talk trash to us. He was a great player, too, had 60-something interceptions as a cornerback. He used to say to me how good he was. He said he would have stopped me in his day. It was funny.

So what's the problem? If it's not the players and it's not the coaches, what do you think? Like I said, I'm cool with Mike Brown. I understand him and he's a good man. He's also a smart man. Really smart. Some people don't think that, but they don't get it. He got that city to build him a stadium and give it all to him. He gets every dime because that city wants to make sure that we have a team.

But he doesn't see what everybody else is doing to win. We don't have a general manager. We have the fewest scouts in the league. Yeah, we have some great players, like me, Carson Palmer, T. J., Levi Jones, Stacy Andrews. But we need more. We need to keep more of the guys we have, like Justin Smith and guys like that. Every time we start to make progress, we go backward. We have Willie Anderson playing and we let him go over a little bit of money.

Look what happens. Willie goes to Baltimore, one of our rivals, and goes to the playoffs. He anchors their line, gets all their young guys to play great, and we struggle. People got on my ass outside the organization because I said our offensive line was struggling. I mean, can't you see what I'm seeing? I'm not ragging on our guys. It's not their fault. But we let go of one of our best guys because of a little bit of money, and we're wondering what happened.

We let go of Rudi Johnson before the season, and then we're going through running backs like crazy. Yeah, we ended up with Cedric Benson, and he's nice. Really nice. He runs hard, man. He was a beast. He had 747 yards in 12 games and he wasn't even ready for the first couple of weeks after he got to us. So really, he's only effective for like 10 games.

I mean, how does that really help us? Yeah, it's nice to pick up a good player during the season, but we could have used somebody good from the beginning before we got in a deep-ass hole.

It's only getting worse, man. Before this off-season, Marvin was talking about how we weren't going to use the franchise tag to keep T. J. It'll take a miracle to get him to come back. He's already talked about wanting to get out and he's tired of everybody thinking he's nothing but a possession receiver. One dink pass after another is all he's been getting the past two years. The dude is frustrated, no question.

We were in the locker room one day and T. J. is talking to Andre Caldwell, a young receiver on the team. T. J. is talking right in front of all the reporters. He doesn't give a shit. He's telling Andre, "I'm telling you, wait till next year when the reporters start saying about you, 'Oh, he's a possession guy.' It's like you can't run anymore." The young receivers were giving T. J. shit about that, and he told them right back how it is. Like I said, he's frustrated with what they do to him. I'd be shocked if he comes back—and there we go again, losing a good player.

But that's the story in Cincinnati when you're a star player. You just get so tired of dealing with the same shit year after year. Look at what happened to Corey Dillon. You know how bad Corey wanted out? He used to tell guys from the other team in the middle of the game, "Hey, man, tell your coach I want to play for you." I'm serious, right in the middle of the game. Think about that. Think about what the guys on the Bengals are thinking when Dillon said that. Some guys used to complain and get all pissed, but I think, "Man, I hope he sticks around, we need him." The dude is getting 1,300 yards a season.

But then Corey has a down year in 2003, gets 541 yards, and it's like they can't wait to get rid of him. Guess what happens? He goes to New England, rushes for 1,635 yards, scores 13 touchdowns, has the best year of his career, and the Patriots win the Super Bowl for the third time in four years.

Why does this happen? It's because Mike Brown doesn't have any real help, he doesn't have enough help. He doesn't trust anybody to tell him, "Hey, we gotta change this." Marvin Lewis wants to help, but all Mike does is tell him to coach. Mike is from a great football family. His old man was Paul Brown, a Hall of Famer, one of the biggest names in the history of the game. His name is on our stadium. The man founded two teams, the Bengals and the Browns. Really, he practically invented the game. I heard he invented the huddle or some shit like that.

So it's not like Mike doesn't know the game. He understands how it works, but this isn't the era his dad coached football in. We need to get real help. I've been here eight years. I've seen it with my own eyes. I've seen how it works. After a while, you start to see where the problems are and you say to yourself, "What can I really do?" At a certain point, it's out of your hands.

It's frustrating, because you want to win so bad and the media is looking at us, the players, because we're the ones out on the field. Hey, we're the only ones answering questions most of the time, so who do you think is going to take the blame for that?

It's like I told Mark Curnutte of the *Cincinnati Enquirer* during the season. At the time, I had like 50 catches through the first 14 games. Fifty catches? Are you freaking kidding me? I should get 50 catches a game. I finished the season with 53 catches, 540 yards, and four touch-downs, which is ridiculous. I could catch 53 balls in my sleep. Hell, I catch that many in one dream.

Man, that got me thinking. Do you think maybe the Bengals will say to themselves, "Hey, Ochocinco only had 540 yards last season, he must be declining"? Then maybe they'll get rid of me. Man, a guy can hope, can't he?

Anyway, so Mark asks me if I'm still feeling confident. I mean, come on, me, not confident? You're kidding.

So I tell him: "I am Chad Johnson. I wear eighty-five and I'm very, very good at what I do." Then Mark reminds me that my last name is now Ochocinco. Good catch by him, so I say: "Yeah, I'm that guy, too. So therefore the numbers will always be what they are. One down year means nothing. . . . Yeah, we're going to bounce back. You want me to guarantee it or just say it? We'll bounce back."

I ended up having the worst season since my rookie year. I had six straight seasons with more than 1,100 yards. Had 90 catches or more in four seasons and 80-something another year. How do I drop to 53 catches? I mean, really, how does that happen?

OK, our quarterback was hurt almost the whole season, I get that part. Carson Palmer played four games before he had to sit out the rest of the season with an elbow injury. He never got better. So we play Ryan Fitzpatrick and he's OK. Really, he was fine, and they could have easily tried to run most of the regular game plan. Look at T. J.'s numbers. Yeah, his yards per catch were down, but he had 90 catches, which is about right.

So what happened with me? Go look at the film. I'm running downfield, waving my arms all season. I'm open. Really, I was. All season. Just look at the film. So what am I to think? I think they're making me pay for all the stuff I said in the off-season. I think somebody upstairs has told them not to throw me the ball.

How else do you explain it? OK, maybe there is some other explanation, but when you get frustrated like I was this season, what am I supposed to think? Seriously, I saw this whole thing coming. I saw how we were going to struggle.

Now, I didn't think I was going to get hurt. I tore the rotator cuff in my right shoulder, so that cost me some time in the exhibition season, but that was no big deal. The doctor said I had a 12-to-6 tear of the shoulder, but that didn't affect me. I could do all the push-ups you could ask for. And it didn't stop me from getting open. Like I said, I was open all season. They just didn't throw me the ball.

But this is what I don't understand. If you're not going to throw to me, why keep me? I even would have given the money back from my contract to get out. I really would have, because I would have gotten a new deal somewhere else. The Bengals could have had the money back. I don't want the money. I want to win.

You want to know how bad it got for me in the 2008 season? When I saw a coach from another team, I was telling them, "Come get me. Save me. I'm going to kill myself if this goes on like this." The coaches from the other teams would just laugh. I bet they thought I was clowning, but I wasn't. I was serious. I just wish it could happen.

Or there's the text messages I traded with Jason Cole, the guy who helped me with this book. We were texting on December 20, as the season was coming to a close.

Me: We suck, the book is gonna end with me killing myself if I have to come back here.

Cole: Reincarnation . . . that could be a bestseller.

Me: I like that, let's do it.

Cole: You'd definitely be comeback player of the year.

Me: Good one.

With Chad everybody is always saying, "Chad wants this or that. Chad is just into himself." Hey, it ain't that. What Chad wants to do is freakin' win, and when he doesn't win, he gets upset and people don't understand. . . . That's why I tell Chad: "Do what you do on the field and then keep your peace with yourself. If you're going through something on that day, you keep that to yourself, you don't need to let everybody in on your thoughts. If it's somebody you need to say that directly to, say it directly to him and then move on."

—**Ray Lewis,** Baltimore Ravens Pro Bowl linebacker

THREE

DON'T BLAME IT ON RAY

THE MAIN PERSON I went to when I was thinking about what I was going to do this off-season, how I was going to try to get out of Cincinnati, was Ray Lewis. Yes, Ray Lewis, the linebacker from Baltimore.

Ray is a smart guy, he's been through a lot, he understands. Yeah, he's wise. He told me to be careful about this. He didn't tell me, go ahead, run your mouth. Ray sees the big picture about the NFL and he can explain it from both sides. He understands where I'm coming from and he understands where the team is coming from. He sees it all. I probably talked to him four or five times, and he kept telling me, "Be careful and do what you think is right."

He just made me think about it. But really, it's how we all are. Yeah, people think this stuff is a war and all and that guys hate each other, but it's really not like that. Yeah, some stuff is serious. Joey Porter and Levi Jones. They ain't playin', something is serious there. Joey Porter and Brandon Marshall? That's serious, although I guess J. P. apologized later. J. P. is a good dude, he just gets a little hyped before games. Too hyped, probably.

Like I'm one to fuckin' talk.

But some people think this team really hates this other team, these guys hate each other and they want to take each other's heads off. And some of that is true. Some guys want to take each other's heads off. I'm the fun guy, I'm just, "Hey, I'm out here having fun." There are other guys, they are literally trying to kill each other.

The thing is that most guys can turn it off right away. That game ends, that play ends, and it's over. Done. That's what fans don't get, probably because so many of them are so pissed off at something. They're not like us, they don't get to take their aggression out for a whole afternoon. If they did, they'd calm the fuck down a lot faster.

See, people don't get that. This is a physical game, and everybody thinks that means we hate each other. Like Hines Ward, when he hit our stud rookie linebacker Keith Rivers, broke the dude's jaw, and knocked him out for the season. That's football and that's no fucking joke. I'm not angry at Hines for doing that. I understand what happens out there. Hines ain't doing that because he wants to hurt the guy, but that's the way you have to play. If it's coming the other way, nobody is saying shit. If Hines goes across the middle and some safety lays him out, that's a good hit. But when Hines does it to a defensive guy, the defensive guys freak the fuck out.

When you play in this league, you better have your head on a swivel, you better be ready, because guys are going to knock you out if they get the chance. I like to run across the middle. There's a lot of plays to make in there, but I know how to get my ass down right away. I can get to the ground quick, and you better know how or somebody is going to be there. Like when [former Cleveland safety] Brian Russell popped me, gave me a concussion. You know what I said? "It was about time somebody got me after all the shit I've talked."

Russell was doing his job, that's all. The next time I saw him before a game, he came up to me and told me how much he appreciated what I said. I said to him, "You really got yours on me, kudos. Now I gotta get mine." That's how it works. That shot is what happens in this game. It was a slant from the right. I think the ball kind of slipped out of Carson's hand, so it sails just a little bit and I gotta go get it. Russell is right there and smacks me. Really, the chances of that happening are pretty small, so if you're a receiver, you just gotta go get it. But be aware that it can happen.

I had a concussion. It happens. I got a couple of stitches, too. That's the way it goes. I was OK that night. I went skating, so it wasn't like I was scared or anything. I didn't even have a headache.

Some guys can turn that on and off. I don't understand how they do it, because I'm not like that. I'm just out having fun, but you better know that guys are going to play that way, and be ready.

It's like with Hines. He's smiling and smiling and smiling at you all game, but if he has to hit you, he's going to knock your ass the fuck out. His hit on Keith Rivers was a good one, the way the game is played. I don't want my guy getting hurt, but that's gonna happen. You have to understand that if you're chasing the runner downfield, the wide receivers are going to come back to help, especially Hines. You got two guys in the open field running at each other at full speed, that shit's going to happen.

Look, that's how Hines makes his money. That's what he has to do, or he's not getting paid by the Steelers. Pittsburgh plays that way, that's their image. If he doesn't play that way, he doesn't have a job. It's not like Hines is one of these guys who just runs away from people all the time. He's a good receiver, but he's not some burner dude who's out there because he can't ever be covered. He's out there because he can catch, he's tough, and he's going to lay it on somebody when he hits them. That's what the Steelers want.

But most of us understand, it's only serious for those 60 minutes every Sunday between those white lines. Away from the field, everybody understands. They get along. We all know it's a business. That's why I can go to a guy like Ray and ask him important questions about what I should do. He understands what we all put into this, what we're all trying to be. Yeah, he may be trying to knock my head off on Sunday, but I can ask him a question about what he thinks is right. He's a guy I can trust.

Ray is the reason I stopped fussing this season when I didn't get traded the way I wanted. When I came to grips with it, when I came to minicamp and they said it's not happening, I just knew. Once I was still here and the minicamp rolled around, I knew it was over, it's a wrap. I took it as far as I could. It was all over. When they turned down those picks from Washington, Philadelphia, and Dallas, I was in tears after that draft. Literally in tears.

That's when I called Ray and talked it through with him. I'd been talking to him all along, but this was serious. I was emotional. I knew I had to go to minicamp, but I was seriously thinking about just saying fuck it. Now, I really wasn't going to do that, but you get frustrated and you gotta talk to somebody.

Ray just said: "If this is what you want to do, do it, but understand the consequences that come behind it and the negative feedback with the media." I told him I was at the point where I really didn't care what people thought. He always reminded me that it's about more than just me. He said, "Think about all the people that wish they were in your shoes, whether you are winning or not. Think about the lesson to be able to play this game whether you are winning or not." He would always finish every sentence "whether you are winning or not." Think about it. Think about the things you can do for your family, for your kids, and all the people here.

Ray and I talked all the off-season and then through the season, when I really started to get it and shut my mouth. In the off-season, I wasn't listening, because I still wanted to get the fuck out of Cincinnati. I was talking to Deion Sanders, too. But mostly Ray. This was the off-season, and he told me to be wise with what I was doing.

Ray is the guy I call when I'm having problems here. It can be half-time of a game, anytime. If something ain't right, call Ray, Deion, or [former Bengals wide receivers coach] Hue Jackson. Those are the people I trust. Ray has always been that one guy I could trust since way back when I played against Baltimore and was crying because I dropped a bunch of balls. That was my second year in the league, and I wanted to beat those guys so bad, show how great I was. He had a talk with me after that game, and we've been close ever since.

I knew him before that, but it was just something different about the way he talked to me after that game. I went to say something to him. I don't remember that conversation that well, but I told him I messed up and he just had some words of encouragement. I don't remember exactly what it was, but ever since then we've been cool. When shit ain't right, he's always got something to say. He's just perfect, he's the first person I talk to when shit ain't right.

With this whole situation with the Bengals and me wanting out of here, he said: "You are going against a beast [NFL management]. This is a system where we are not designed to win." That's the message in so many words. We're not designed to win or battle the system. We're supposed to be a part of it, that's all, not go against it, not be above it, but be just a small piece of what's going on. Sometimes you think to yourself, "That's frustrating," but that's where Ray keeps saying, "Think about all the people that want to be in your shoes."

Again, it's about taking care of more than just yourself. That's why when I was thinking about not coming to minicamp, I looked at my contract and said I'm not going to play my money like that. I worked too hard. It's a game and the owners always win, regardless.

That's what Ray got me to understand, and he helps so many guys. Everybody in the league talks to Ray to get advice on how to handle things. He absorbs so much. He thinks the way the owners think up top and thinks the way we think as players also. Our minds don't work the same way as the system does.

RAY LEWIS

Baltimore Ravens Pro Bowl linebacker

I understand and I give my time, because I owe it. I owe it, owe it, and owe it. I look at it this way: If God gives you the ability to do something great, sometimes he takes you through the ups and downs, the highs, the lows. A lot of the time if you go through those things, it's not even for you. A lot of time it's for you to pass it on and educate somebody else. That's what I have learned, even in this business. In this AFC Championship Game [against Pittsburgh in the 2008 season] and throughout the whole season, one word I kept out of our locker room was "disappointment." There's no way this thing is disappointment when you go out and give everything you've got. You take what comes with it, because at the end of the day there's going to be a winner and a loser, and that's just a fact of life about our business. You have to take those same concepts in regular life. Whatever decisions you make in life, make them, but understand the consequences that come with the decisions. That's the kind of thing I try to educate guys about.

That's where Chad is having a problem, because he's not winning. He's frustrated, and that's what happens to the great ones. All great ones do [want to win]. All of them. I can name numerous cases from the beginning of time all the way to here like that. But sometimes when you find yourself in situations like that, the best thing you can do is keep your peace. That's the thing I tried to impress upon him, try to challenge him with. You see, we've all seen disgruntled players go through this just because they're losing. Not because they're a bad person, but because they are the greatest competitors ever and they want to win so bad. That's the thing I try to channel him to do by telling him, "Hey, everybody don't need to know what you're thinking, even if you're thinking it." It's something about controlling your tongue. That's the biggest thing I told him about last year. I said, "Whether you realize it or not, me and you are in similar situations."

I'm in a situation where I was going into the last year of my contract and I could say anything I want to.

But why? Why? Check it with God, keep it between your players, and everything will take care of itself. These were the things I would work on with Chad constantly. Hold that rage. Keep that emotion. Don't give it to everybody. But sometimes before I would talk to him, he'd give it away. So now what's the counter? That's what we would talk about. How are we going to come back through it? We're in it, how do we get out? That's my thing about all these guys. If you're in something or you're about to be in something, or even if you think you're in something, how are you going to deal with it? That's why I talk to all these guys. I try to give them the flip side of things. If you do whatever you're thinking about, what can happen? That's what I do.

Fans may think that's weird, that maybe it somehow takes away from Sunday. But you know what? Sundays are kind of easy, because you've got like an excuse to just go play football. If you gotta hit somebody, you gotta hit somebody on Sunday, because it's your job. I don't care what your job is, you're going to get up and do your job. That's it. If it's on Sunday, that's it. Once Sunday is set aside, life truly kicks in. Life, regular issues, they kick in. All of us have regular issues, and that's the way it's going to be. So now it's the everyday balance for me to pick up a phone call, text these young guys on why they shouldn't do such and such, tell them why they should stay focused on the things they have to do. Some days, I sit on my computer and I watch film and I sit on the phone for four or five hours talking to different guys.

That's Monday, Tuesday, Wednesday, Thursday, Friday, Saturday, all the way up to game time. Some guys I even talk to all the way up to Sunday morning, right before the game. Whatever it is. Whether it's get your mind right before the game, clear things out of your head, or "Hey, man, I just gotta talk to you, there are a lot of things going on." I say, "Hey, whatever it is, call me after the game, this is what I need you to focus on right now." So it's like Monday through Saturday you just gotta kind of move yourself aside and let all these other guys in. What's amazing is how many guys call [me]. It's amazing, and it's amazing how many are looking for [some help]. But we have to ask ourselves, how many guys are really OK with always sharing, always giving away? Some guys say, "Hey, I don't have time." Man, I've got to. I have to because I owe these kids a lot.

And yeah, that's important to me, because this game has given me so much and I have to set an example so that other guys will do the same. With Chad, we had a lot of talks, but it was gratifying. When we got to Tampa [for the events before the Super Bowl in 2009], I saw him at this Pepsi promotion that we had. It was just a look that we had. We were playing this game, and I was talking to him and said, "Hey, what'd we talk about in the off-season?" And we recapped every-thing we talked about, and as soon as we were done the first thing he said was, "You was right, again." This is the thing, it's like a father to a child, you appreciate it. It's men leaning on you to grab something, and to see Chad use effort to grab it, that's satisfying.

I just think it's an unbelievable story and how fortunate Chad is to be where he is when you understand what he grew up in and how he went so many different places. And yet to have a sense about him in some ways . . . that's beyond his years. And, in other ways, he's just the little kid at heart always looking for more attention. It's a very complex range.

—**Marvin Lewis,** Cincinnati Bengals head coach

FOUR

COACHING OCHOCINCO

PEOPLE THINK I CAN'T be handled, that coaches hate me and don't want to work with me. Whatever, people don't understand. I love my coaches. If it wasn't for Bengals offensive coordinator Bob Bratkowski, I wouldn't be in the NFL. Hell, I might not have the success I've had without him knowing how to use me, how to work with me. Serious. We met at the Senior Bowl when I was coming out of Oregon State, and after he got to the Bengals, he pushed for them to draft me.

You want to know how much I love my coaches, how much I feel I owe them? I was ready to give them $100,000 when I wasn't playing well. That's how much. For real. All you have to do is ask Bratkowski. Coach Brat knows, because I freaked him out one day in 2003.

We played Buffalo in the fifth game of the year that season. I had a shitty game. Six catches, 59 yards, didn't make any impact. I was pissed.

It was my third season. I'd been really good my second year and was ready to break out that season. But I sucked that game.

So on Tuesday, that's the day that the coaches are in the offices and the players are off, I came in. I wasn't supposed to, but I came in to where the offensive coaches were meeting and I told those guys how bad I played. And then I handed Brat a blank check made out for $100,000. He was sitting there with like five other coaches.

Then I told them: "If I don't play up to my ability the rest of the season, you guys can keep the money. If I play up to what you think, then you can give me the check back." Brat told me I couldn't do that, I had to keep the check, he couldn't take it. I told him, keep the damn check. I'm serious. We go back and forth, and finally I just toss the check at him and walk out.

BOB BRATKOWSKI
Cincinnati Bengals offensive coordinator

I'm not sure he earned it back. I'm kidding, a little. But it's like with everything with Chad, there's never a dull moment. I'm just looking at this check and thinking, "What am I supposed to do about this?" The coaches, we just look at each other after he leaves and we shake our heads. This one was a beauty. I was scared out of my mind that I might lose it.

Finally, I decided to put my name on it and then take it home and hide it away. That way, I figured, if somebody stole it, they'd also have to prove they were me. So the season comes to an end and I get the check and give it back to Chad, and he didn't even remember writing it to me or bringing it in the office. But that's Chad. . . .

He is the most unique personality I have been around in this profession. I've been with him every step of the way in the NFL. I've seen every practice, every game, every play since he came into the league.

Brat is telling the truth right there. Hell, I thought I was going to be a first-round pick. I thought everybody wanted me, that I was going in the top 10. But then I spent draft day watching pick after pick after pick go by. Eventually, I just went in a room by myself at my grandmother's house in Miami after the second round started. I ended up in the second round with the Bengals, but only because Brat stood up for me.

Coach Hue Jackson, my old wide receivers coach with Cincinnati who's with Baltimore now, is one of my closest friends. He's one of the guys I trust. I love him. People think I took a swing at him in that play-off game we had against Pittsburgh. That's ridiculous. Yeah, I was hyped for that game and I got emotional. But I didn't swing at anybody. My problem is that I had two catches in the first half and we're hanging on. My problem is that I'm not getting the ball and I'm trying everything I can to win this game. When I don't get the goddamn ball, it fucking pisses me off. It's worse than my dad not being there, if you don't throw me the ball. It'll be smoke in the city. That's what Terrell Owens says. He doesn't curse. That's when you know he's pissed off, he says, "It's going to be smoke in the city."

Yeah, they had to restrain me, but I was just excited. I wasn't going to fight with anybody, I just wanted to make sure they knew what I thought about how to win this game. It's our biggest game and I gotta do what I can do to win this game. That's all I'm thinking. I gotta do whatever. Now, whoever said I swung at someone, they just don't know. They don't understand. It's not like I was Shaun Smith taking a swing at Brady Quinn in Cleveland. I mean, taking a swing at your quarterback? Yeah, Shaun's a genius. That'll help him keep a job.

Same goes with Marvin Lewis, our head coach. I love Marvin. I get along with Marvin. I call him all the time, talk to him about what we're doing. He calls me and wants to know what I'm thinking.

But if you don't believe me, talk to my coaches. Or just read what they have to say. Here goes:

MARVIN LEWIS
Cincinnati Bengals head coach

Hey, it's a ride with Chad. Sometimes he's up here [Lewis puts his hand above his head] and sometimes he's down here [Lewis puts his hand around his knee]. Chad is work, but the one thing you always know is that he wants to be great. He wants to be the best at what he does. He doesn't always know how to get there, but that's what my job is, to tell him how to get there and get him to trust that what I'm saying is true and real.

When I first got to Cincinnati, I really had no idea of who Chad Johnson was and what he was about. When I took the job, I really had no idea. Same thing with T. J. Houshmandzadeh, our other wide receiver, didn't know anything about them other than they were talented, productive guys. Shortly after I got here in 2003, I took those guys with me to a school to visit, a Play It Smart program. You're supposed to get up and talk to kids and tell them about yourself, your story of how you got to where you are.

So I said to Chad and T. J., "Have you guys done any of this before?" They said no and asked if they were going to have to tell their story. I said, "Why don't you practice on me?" So Chad began to tell the story about high school, and going from high school to high school and junior college to junior college and getting six weeks or ten weeks at Oregon State, whatever it was. I'm sitting there thinking, "OK, this is going to be interesting for the kids to unravel." But that's what Chad has had to deal with his whole life to get where he is. It's not a stable life where you can say, "Oh yeah, I can follow that along logically." Chad is very smart, but he's different.

It's like the time I met his mom, his real mom, for the first time. She just has this way about her that kind of takes you off guard. You can see she's sharp, really intelligent, but really guarded. So you're not sure what to expect out of that conversation as it's going along. It was very abrupt. I didn't know what to expect. I think it's one of those situations where you'd have to work to get her to trust you. In some ways, Chad is the same way. He's more open, but he's not necessarily trusting. He's checking you out all the time.

Like I said, he can have some mood swings, he really can. So you gotta try to look ahead and see him coming and really try to cut him off, because a lot of how things go depends on him. He has been a lot of the momentum or inertia behind the locomotive at times. His energy and his passion come out. I think [the 2008 season] has been a tough year on him because he shed some negative light on himself with asking for the trade, and then he gets injured and so things don't go right. He had these great expectations of what he wanted and that didn't happen. Then, when you're out in front of the public like that, it brings even more pressure on you and then you're not forgiven by people for all the things that go wrong that you may not be able to control.

This season has been hard. He's had to maintain himself, and it starts from the whole thing in the off-season to him needing the ankle surgery to hurting his shoulder in training camp to the whole name-change thing. It's one thing to another, both physical and mental. Then the fact that we are not having the success on the field, partly because he realized that we weren't in position to do some of the things he's good at and he's failed to do because he didn't have the time in practice, and then he's been injured. It's been tough.

When he says he calls at three or four in the morning, he's not lying. All times during the day, the night. He is like having a second son. It's, for the most part, positive. Maybe it's too strong to say I'm a parent to him, but hopefully he will look back and say that there have been things that I've helped him with in his life. That would be good. That would be meaningful to me. Hopefully, I've helped him become a better man, that he becomes a better father, and a better husband, some of those things, as well as a football player. But I hope that those things off the field that are important—he has a lot of responsibility off the field—hopefully, there are things we have been able to steer him in the right direction with.

I don't agree with a lot of the things he does, and he knows that. So those things he keeps away from me. If I find out something that he's going to do that's out of the norm and it's not going to be taken the right way, I tell him that. I say, "If you do that, this is the way people are going to look at you." Most of it comes out of the responsibility of whether I can do something or not other than just flat sitting him out. He practices hard, plays hard, you've gotta correct him. Sometimes it's hard on him taking correction, and that's the part that he's had to work through.

But it is important to him. He wants to be good, to be great, and he wants to win. I think he does recognize the fact that without the success of the football team, success for him off the field isn't going to be the same. He's not going to be viewed in the same light. The reason he grew to what he grew to was the success that the football team had. He was part of that success. Now when we're not doing well, he's looked at the other way, like he's somehow the problem. But that's because he brought so much attention on himself.

Now, he loves the lights and spotlight and the attention, and that drives him, and that's a good thing. I think everybody is motivated by certain things. I think that he is driven by the attention of success and so forth that comes from it, and is just channeling it all in the right direction all the time. Channeling that takes a lot of management skill, and there are times that I sit there and think, "Don't do that." Like I said, if I find out about it, I guide him to a better decision. If I don't, well . . . it's like the time he wore the Hall of Fame jacket. To me that was the one, I wish he would have never done that. I wish I would have gotten wind of that before and we could have nipped it in the bud. We tried to talk him out of the name change, obviously with no success. But the Hall of Fame coat thing, if there was one thing that I wished I could have found out about beforehand . . .

To me, he is a very good player. Having been fortunate enough in my coaching career to be around these Hall of Fame guys like Lynn Swann, Terry Bradshaw, or Mel Blount, Joe Montana, Rod Woodson, I know how important the game was to them and to not be presumptuous about it. How sacred that is to the NFL and the players and the coaches. There are a lot of good players that don't make it into the Hall of Fame, and there are a lot of great players who have to wait a long time to get in. Look at Swann. It wasn't easy for him. You're talking about guys who were not only good players, they were successful people.

To me, that jacket incident was presumptuous and shed a negative light on Chad that he didn't need and didn't deserve. In some way, it might hurt him from getting there if he's worth discussing by the end of his career, when it's all said and done. Do you want that image out there? Do you want to fight that to get in when it's already so hard for some guys to get in?

This is hard enough to do when you're just dealing with the stuff that people make up. It's like when people talk about the "fight" that happened [during the playoff game]. People made a big deal about nothing. There was no fight. Chad jumped off the IV table. There was blood dripping out of him because he had an IV in him and that's it. Anybody who knows Chad knows he can't swing at anybody because they might swing back.

Unfortunately, people lied about that and the story grew, because that's how people are. They want to be cynical, and they want to be cutting, and there are people that don't like Chad stealing their thun-der. Those guys all left this football team last year because they were just—there's a jealousy that comes and it's just bad. That's the thing, that it was just unfortunate. Was Chad upset? Yeah, he was upset, everybody was upset. Is he going to swing at his coach? No, he's not going to swing at his position coach, and he's certainly not ever going to swing at me. That's the part that no one understands. If he had swung at Hue Jackson or me, he wouldn't have been out there in the second half of the game, point-blank. That's the thing people don't un-derstand. That's why it was so far-fetched to say.

The thing that he needs to understand most is that he's been rel-atively healthy in his career until this past season. Over the last cou-ple of years, he has had to learn how to deal with injury and pain. Prior to having his ankle cleaned out, frankly, some days he would practice and the next day he would be very, very sore. He saw other guys getting more time off because they were injured. They were pulled out of things where he wanted to back out of it the same way. You are pushing him, and he would take offense at that because he wanted to be treated that same way as the others. Sometimes I have to get in his face because you need him doing the work, at least part of the work, the work we felt like he needed to have to be ready on Sunday. In my judgment, it was better for him to get part of the work than none of the work.

That's part of him. I'm sure there are some professional golfers that can pick up the club and go play. And there are others that prac-tice five hours a day every day they are not on the field. He's one of those guys who is used to practicing. He's used to it, whether he needs it or not, that's his routine. That's how he does it, and that's what makes him special, how hard he works.

It's like when people talk about his body control. He has been very, very good at it and, fortunately, we're trying to get back to that point. I think the shoulder injury, the whole off-season situation, just not having the time on task. I think everyone [on the team] took for granted that in March, early April, [Chad and T. J.] would come up to my office and say, "Why can't we go out and throw?" That didn't happen this year. They were always chomping at the bit to go to work and to practice. I think when you take away a little bit of that, you take a little bit of what he was, what he had been. He recognizes that going forward.

HUE JACKSON

former Cincinnati Bengals wide receivers coach

Marvin is right about how Chad can be so up one day and down the next. That's just Chad. I never took it personally with him, it was just how he'd be. Sometimes he'd come into a receivers meeting with his sweatshirt hood over his head, not looking at anybody, and some days he'd be jumping off the top of the desks. Sometimes you had to bring him out of whatever state he was in.

But what he always has is a burning desire to be the best receiver he can be, the best receiver in the NFL. He wants to be out front, right there as the best, and he soaks up whatever you can give him to help him be that great player, that supreme wide receiver. People call wide receivers prima donnas because so many of them talk about being great and say they're this and that. Let me tell you, there's not one of them worth their salt who doesn't think that if he gets the ball, he's going to make enough plays to win the game. That's just what they are. They have to have the ball. They need the ball to live, to exist.

What people don't understand is that there's a fine line with wide receivers. When it's about getting the ball to win the game, that's fine. When it becomes about being selfish and just about how you need your numbers, that's where it affects other guys to the point where those guys don't want to be around you. Chad doesn't cross that line. The guys want to be in there with him. He's a fun-loving guy, a prankster, a jokester, a child in his own way, but the guys know where his head is at. You can put it this way: There's a bad selfishness and a good selfishness, and guys know the difference, whether they can explain it or not. If it's that you want to be the guy to help the team win, that's OK. If you're just counting numbers, no.

Chad wants to prove he's the best at what he does, and sometimes it comes off wrong to the public. In his mind, he doesn't need to explain himself, because people on the team understand. He thinks everybody else should understand as well. Look at all the great receivers, from Terrell Owens to Randy Moss to T. J. Houshmandzadeh to Chad to Marvin Harrison. What good receiver doesn't want the ball, doesn't think he can turn a game around by himself? When those guys have to block for a whole quarter and all of a sudden they can feel the ship going the other way, they get anxious. They can't see the double or triple coverage. They're blind to it because in their mind they think they can beat every double team. They think they're always open.

Chad talks about how the defensive backs are invisible to him. That's exactly what he believes. They're not there, therefore he must be open every play. And the football to these guys is like their medicine in the game. They thrive on getting the ball. If they don't touch the ball early in a game, they're off their game, and the longer they go without the ball, the harder it is to get them in a rhythm.

I really didn't understand that until I got around Chad. I was a high school and college quarterback and I've coached since 1987. I've coached running backs, quarterbacks, and been an offensive coordinator, but I hadn't been a wide receivers coach until I got to Cincinnati in 2004. Being around those guys, Chad and T. J., I got it. I understood what having to have the ball really meant. It's not about making them happy, it's about making them part of the game. I was really missing it until Chad was around me, catching 85–90 balls, 1,300 yards, eight or nine touchdowns a season. That sounds easy, but it's hard to do that every single year. He led the AFC in receiving yards four straight years. Nobody had ever done that before.

But he's in a competition with himself to leave a legacy as the best receiver to ever play the game. I've never seen him as a bad teammate. Can he do things better? Sure, he could block better. He knows that. He's done things in the process of us teaching him to be better at that. But I'll be honest with you about the blocking: As a coach, I'm not really worried about that. Yeah, you want it and it helps, but I need receivers who can go get the ball, who can change a game with a big catch or a run after the catch, and that's what Chad can do. His ability to catch does way more to open up the running game than any number of blocks he can throw, and that's the truth.

People say he's soft, but they don't get it. They don't look at his body and understand he's a skinny guy. Chad ain't going to go up and hit Troy Polamalu, and that's a business decision. If he tries to do that he knows, "If I go in and make that block and crash pads against these big dudes, I'm knocking my shoulder out for this and I'm going to be down for six weeks." We have a guy who can catch 85 or 90 balls and we're worried about one block? Come on.

And you have to get him going that way. The ball fuels him to go be a better player. It's like taking a baby's pacifier away. If you don't get a great receiver the ball, they're all out of sorts. The playoff game against Pittsburgh is a classic example. Chad got two catches in the first half, but we're still not able to throw to him that much. We throw the ball 21 times, but the biggest play comes on the first throw by Carson Palmer, when we hit Chris Henry for 66 yards. That's the play where we lose Carson with the knee injury. The rest of the half, it's almost all short stuff, six yards here, eight yards there. We can't get free, we can't get big plays to Chad. Pittsburgh won't let us and that's not how Jon Kitna plays. Kitna is a good player and he helped us through a lot of years, but he's not Carson and that's that.

We've got a 17–14 lead at halftime, but you can sense that the game is shifting, Pittsburgh has the momentum, so we're trying to fig- ure out a plan for the second half, and it means that Chad's probably not going to get the ball much more. [Note: Ochocinco finished the game with four catches for 59 yards total.]

Chad hears that, he's so hyped from the first half that he's on an IV, and now he's acting out about what we need to do. I tell him he needs to go talk to the guys in charge if he doesn't like it, so he jumps up with the IV in his arm and starts going over to talk to the rest of the coaches. It's a scene now, but you have to understand, that's how much he believes he can impact a game.

Did he swing at me? Hell, no. He knows better than that. He knows what I'd do. It's sad that it came out that way in some reports, but it wasn't like that. Nobody had anybody in a headlock or threw a punch or anything like that. It never happened. He wanted the ball and people thought he was selfish. He just wanted to win the game. It's no different than when everybody saw Minnesota running back Adrian Peterson getting all angry at the end of a game because he was being taken out on third-and-1. Great players want to be in the game at those big moments. They trust themselves, and you have to understand that.

In that playoff game, Carson was out of the game and we're doing what we had to do. Remember, this is the first playoff game of Chad's career. He was really amped up, he wanted to win so bad. Plus, we're playing Pittsburgh, and he doesn't think there's any defensive back that can cover him on that team. That's the way he is.

You just have to know that he's fueled by challenges to be great. My first year there, in 2004, there was a game we had against Buffalo late in the season and Nate Clements, the Bills cornerback, just controlled Chad the whole game. Chad had two catches for 10 yards, his worst game by far. Clements was all up in him all game. It was unreal.

So I told Chad during the game that Clements owned him that day. We got our ass kicked 33–17 and I told Chad, "You stunk today." He had two touchdowns the next week, and that fueled him all of 2005, when we made the playoffs. When we played Buffalo and Nate Clements again in 2005, Chad was the best player on the field. He had nine catches, 117 yards, and a touchdown. He was unreal. When challenged, he's going to respond. There's no candle to burn out with him, but you do have to know how to challenge him. It can be stories on television, news stories, winning edges, whatever, you have to challenge him and keep the fear in him that maybe he's slipping, that he's not the best. As soon as you do that, watch out. The guy can play with the best of them. He needs an environment that allows him to be him, and the most important thing is he needs to touch that ball.

With him at practice, yeah, sometimes I had to put my foot up his ass. There's a specific way I want practice run, and I want it done that way every day. One day, he was half-assing it. He said he wasn't warmed up or something, and I thought he was ready to go. So I was real specific with him. He said something back to me and it got tense. There were nasty words going back and forth. Hey, if he wants to fight about it, I wanted to fight about it. But he's like my son that way. Sometimes you have to put your foot up their ass to get what you need. I want perfection. I'm not interested in him just running around, jogging through practice half-assed. He got frustrated and mad and I got frustrated and mad, and we were ready to go at it. That's fine, that's how it has to be sometimes.

BOB BRATKOWSKI
Cincinnati Bengals offensive coordinator

I was coaching with the Pittsburgh Steelers at the time [in 2001] and our staff was working the Senior Bowl that year. I coached the receivers and I had Chad on our team. Later on, I got hired by Cincinnati. But I remember working with Chad that week. I had a chance to work with him all week and get to know him. Here's a guy who had just been at Oregon State for one year. But everybody was saying he's a one-year wonder in college. He couldn't stay eligible anywhere he'd been, he was one year here, one year there, he had no track record.

But I sat down with him one day and asked him about it. He looked at me and said: "I don't drink, I don't smoke, I absolutely love football, and I hate school. I can't stand going to class." That whole week, he showed exactly what he was talking about. He wanted to learn the whole time, pick up everything he could. When I got to the Bengals and we had a chance to get him, I told them exactly what I thought. I believed what he said. I trusted him and he was telling the truth. He doesn't like class. But he has a passion for the game. Early in his career, he was better than he is now about wanting to learn everything and spend extra hours in the office. Now he thinks he has everything down, when there's really some finer things about the game he could be learning.

He still has a terrible time sitting still and staying focused in a meeting. He'll have short bursts where he can stay focused, and then he gets antsy, and it's worse now that he thinks he knows it all. It's harder to keep his attention. He gets bored faster. You have to find ways to challenge him and keep his attention. At the same time, you have to work through stuff with everyone, so there's this constant push and pull to how you work with him.

The thing is that he is exceptionally bright. You can see where his mind is moving all the time, especially if it's a day where he comes in with really high energy. He's bright and he's quick-witted. There are things he'll come up with that are hilarious. Things that are just in the moment, observations about something that's going on or something that happened, a situation that we're going over. We were out at practice one day and he looked at one of the players and noticed that the guy looked a lot like Justin Timberlake. Nobody else had noticed, but he did, and all of sudden he's calling out, "Hey, Timberlake." He's always coming up with nicknames for guys, breaking people up. At times, he can be the class clown. He has gotten up in front of the team and told jokes, some of them go over big, some days they really don't, but he'll have that energy to put himself up in front of everybody.

I don't think there's any doubt that he wants to win, and win very badly. But his actions don't always back that up. In critical situations, he has scored a touchdown and then done some ridiculous celebration that gets us a penalty and all of a sudden we're kicking off from way back in our own territory. That's what he does from time to time. He doesn't think about what we have to get accomplished at that moment. That's where you think, "Chad, are you really concerned about winning?" If winning is really the number-one thing, you don't allow those situations to happen, you don't allow the "It's About Me" stuff to override the things you have to do to win games.

The same goes for blocking. He has never been a great blocker, and Hue is right, he's not very physical. That's not what he does. But at times he has shied away from it, and on great teams, the wide receivers make critical blocks downfield to help the running game. You can't just jump out of the way sometimes and let the running back get hit. Nobody expects him to be a killer, but you have to do more than what he has done. We've all worked really hard to help him go the full way with his talent, to strive to get it out of him. You look at his body of work and he has done some great things, but the truly great players, they have that body of work that includes being on teams that made the playoffs a lot. You look at them and you see how many championships they have won, and then you look at Chad's body of work and we're still trying to get there. We still have to address things, you can't just brush it under the carpet and hide them there.

I love him like a son, and that's why I say these things. I've been close to him the entire time he's been here, that we've been here. But I would tell him he's leaving things out there he could be better at. That's what drives you crazy as a coach. You want him to be fully maxed out of his potential, and getting him to do that is a never-ending battle. And because he's so bright and so quick and so emotional, pushing the right buttons to get it out of him is always different. With most guys, it's pretty easy. You say something to them and you have a pretty good idea how they're going to respond. With Chad, he's very hard to approach at times. Sometimes you have to try a very soft, kind of cajoling manner. Sometimes I've called him out in front of the whole team. Sometimes I've called him in privately and appealed to his pride. They have all been effective at times, and at other times not effective at all. It's a constant monitoring process. He has tremendous pride, and sometimes you want to appeal to that and sometimes you want to be careful with it, because you can lose him.

He's just a really interesting guy in that way, because the way he was raised was very different and how he got here was different. He's unique. His grandmother did a lot of work in raising him. At the same time, he was raised with no real father figure in his life for a long time. All of those things add up to it, to a person who is very interesting.

I came home one day and I hadn't seen my daughter, Chad's mother, for a couple of days. Chad was about four or five at the time. I asked Chad, "Where is your mother?" He looked up at me and said, "She went to Los Angeles with Chauncey." Chauncey is Chad's little brother.

—**Bessie Mae Flowers,** Chad's grandmother

FIVE

GROWIN' UP

I DON'T REALLY TALK to my father very much. He lives in Liberty City, which is where I grew up. It's a little part of Miami on the north side of town. He's somewhere around there. I don't see him much and he was never around when I was a kid. We don't have much of a relationship. I really don't care.

I really don't. Yeah, you might care. I hear people talk about that stuff all the time. What was it like to not have your dad around, or people talk about what their dad was like and what I must have missed. To me, it doesn't matter. He didn't raise me. He didn't put in any effort. When I made it to the NFL, I heard from him. A little late, whatever. That happens to a lot of guys in the NFL. They make it big-time and all of a sudden the daddy they never knew shows up and expects everything to be all good.

Just look around. Plaxico Burress didn't meet his dad till he was in college. Terrell Owens didn't know his dad until he was like 12. Steve

Smith was raised by his mom. Those guys handled it, they made it. What makes me so special that I should be complaining about not having my dad around? Hey, what's the big deal? Really, it's his loss. Hey, if he didn't want to be around, so be it. He didn't want to put in the time, so I go my way.

The thing for me is that I'm not going to be like that. Yeah, I have four kids with three women. I didn't marry any of them. Some people look at that as all wrong, that I must be a bad father. I take good care of my kids, I spend time with them when I'm back in Miami. I bring my son, he lives out in Los Angeles, out to see me. They get time with me, they know who I am. I support them. That's what I'm supposed to do. That's what a dad is supposed to do.

But we'll get into that more later. This is about how I was raised and what it means to me. I'm not going to sit here and cry about what I didn't get or say, "Oh, my daddy wasn't here, that's why I do this or do that." I am what I am. I'm having fun and I work hard. The people around me were the influences on my life. And for those people who think I'm weird or whatever, think about this:

I don't drink, I don't smoke, I don't do drugs, I've never been arrested since I got to the NFL. I don't have a bunch of off-field problems. You don't see the police coming to my house. Doesn't happen. So did not having my dad around make me something really bad or evil? No. That's because I don't worry about that. It wasn't about me. It was about him. I'm not wasting much time thinking about it.

I'm pretty much the same way with my mother. Paula Johnson is her name. People think my mom looks like me. She even has her head basically shaved like mine. Same kind of facial expression, and she's moody. I see her more often. She's around from time to time, living at my grandmother's house or wherever. Sometimes she's in New York. For a long time she was living in Los Angeles. But we don't really talk, either. Just doesn't happen. I don't even have her phone number.

My grandmother, Bessie Mae Flowers, raised me mostly, but my mom (she's Bessie Mae's daughter), she is a little different now. My mom was wild, out of control. When I was born, she couldn't take care of me. My mom, though, when we would be together, it was different. She can talk some trash. Her mouth never stops moving. With my mom, you basically have to get into it with her to be accepted. It's like the initiation to the group. My mom is going to challenge you to see if you're going to stand up or just take it. If you just take it, she's going to ride you.

Like one time when I was little, I was in the car with her and we're trying to park at the grocery store. This is down in Miami, probably back in the 1980s. We're at Publix or something and some other lady cuts my mom off as she's trying to park her car. My mom gets out of the car and she just lets the other lady have it. She's yelling and screaming this and that, just cursing this lady out.

Then my mom grabs the lady's keys and pulls the other car out, gets back in her car, and parks her car in the spot. The other lady never said a word. Hey, my mom can be totally wild. Totally out there.

Like I said, my grandmother was the one who raised me. Her and her second husband, James Flowers, who I look at as my grandfather. They're the ones who took care of me. I call my grandmother "Mommy" because she's the one who took care of me the most. I spent some time with my mom from time to time, but my grandmother is the one who really raised me. It's not like that's some big deal. That's what lots of guys in the NFL deal with, so that's why I say I don't care. I really don't. You think what I had was so much different?

It's like when people ask how hard I work to stay in shape to play in the NFL and I don't ever tell them. Everybody in the NFL works hard. If you don't, you don't last. That's just the way it is. Just like how I grew up. That's the way it is.

We lived in a corner house in Liberty City. My grandmother is still there. It's a nice house, especially compared to the rest of the neighborhood. She's got a fountain in the front yard and a short fence around the lot. It has a fake iron gate thing attached to the fence. And she has bars on the windows. She's been broken into once. Hey, it's a nice house and the street is OK. She has cops living around her.

But it's still Liberty City. This ain't a middle-class neighborhood. You can figure that out by the pack of stray dogs roaming the neighborhood and the bars on just about all the windows. There's no big chain supermarket nearby, not something nice like Publix. Most of the stores, at least the ones that are still open, are what we call "package" stores, where they sell alcohol and other small stuff. There's Martin Luther King Jr. Boulevard, and then there's Obama murals everywhere.

Yep, Liberty City is the black neighborhood. That's how it was designed back in 1930, when they opened the Liberty Square Housing Project, the only place for blacks to live in what was then pretty much all-white Miami. It's about a four-mile-by-four-mile stretch of town. Right next door to the west is Hialeah and Miami Springs. That's mostly Hispanic now, and pretty much was already when I was growing up.

The border on the east side of the city is I-95, which basically is this big wall except for a few spots where you can drive under the freeway and head to the water. They didn't even give the black people any waterfront property back then. To this day the city is like 95 percent black, and if you check the history you find the biggest events are about violence. We had the Liberty City Riots in 1980, before I could really remember anything. That was about five white cops who got off after chasing some black guy on a motorcycle and then beating him to death. One of the cops even admitted it on the stand, and they still got off.

Then, in 1998, we had a famous gang war over drug territory. Some dude tried to take over the John Does gang, some shit like that. A couple of years ago, they had another rash of shootings related to drugs. I wonder how Grand Theft Auto got the idea.

I'm kidding.

We have some pretty famous people from Liberty City, too. Udonis Haslem from the NBA played at Northwestern High School, which is right there. The rappers Trick Daddy and Luther Campbell are from there. We have actors, singers, athletes, all sorts of artists.

I've tried to get my grandmother to move out of there, but she won't. She always says, "What for?" I'm like, "Because that house is old and beat up and the neighborhood is bad." But she won't go. I'd buy her a nice place up near me in Davie, but she won't. She wants money to fix that house and I just think that's a waste.

I still hang out there quite a bit, come by and say what up to the guys I grew up with, the ones who are still around. My room in her house is the same as when I grew up, and that's where I got my dream that I was going to play football. That room had wallpaper with the pennants from all the NFL teams when I was growing up. I'd just look at the names of the teams and think, "That's what I'm going to do."

The good thing for me is I wasn't part of that crime stuff. My grandmother wouldn't have it. I was either goofing around at school, playing football, or I was home. That's it. She didn't put up with any foolishness. She wouldn't have it. That's why I'm lucky and one of the reasons I made it. She put so much effort into making sure I didn't do stupid things.

And I got my ass whupped all the time. All the time. I remember one time my grandmom and my grandfather went to church. He had a Mercedes-Benz. I took the car and pulled it out the driveway and got the right fender caught because I didn't know how to drive yet. I got the right fender caught on the edge of the gate. So I thought if I keep going, it will free itself up. Man, I ripped the whole right side from the front wheel to the front bumper, ripped it right off. I was scared to death, and I just left it there, so when they got home, oh man. My granddaddy beat the shit out of me. I will never forget. That was the worst whipping I ever had. I think that might have been my last time getting in trouble, for real. I think that ass-whupping did it. My eyes closed and I saw the light, and something said, "Don't go bad." I saw the light. I was done being bad.

It's like alcohol and drugs. I don't drink. I've never tried weed, drugs, never tried none of that. It surrounds me. It's everywhere, and people outside of what I do, everybody does a little bit of everything. I ain't going to lie. They do a little bit of everything, still to this day. There are guys in the league who do stuff, we all know that. But I've never been like that. Never interested. If I did get busted, they'd probably say: "I knew something was wrong with that motherfucker, as crazy as he is."

When I was growing up, I never had problems with fighting and stuff. Not at all. It was all sports and video games. I think with fighting, what is there for me to fight about back then? You step on my shoes? No, I don't care. Over a girl? Yeah, right, it ain't happening.

My grandfather was a good man. Came to my youth practices, my games, helped out. He used to warn me all the time about what parts of the neighborhood to stay out of. Don't cross 12th Avenue, don't go here, don't go there. It kind of sucks, because even though he told me all the time, he ended up being in the wrong place. He separated from my grandmother at one point and then somebody shot him at a party he was at when I was in high school. Nobody ever found out who did it. That's the way it goes in Liberty City.

But the thing my grandmother did most was make sure I wasn't part of that scene growing up in Liberty City. I didn't play sports in that neighborhood. I didn't go to the school in that neighborhood, Miami Northwestern, one of the football powerhouses in Florida. I had some friends from there, but I was always driving around, doing something else, playing somewhere else. She made sure of that. Heck, I played Pop Warner football in Miami Lakes, this middle-class neighborhood like 45 minutes away from my house. That's how much she made sure I wasn't part of that.

My grandmom was very strict, she raised me. She was so strict it was ridiculous. For one, she was a teacher in school, so that's like your mom or your dad being the sheriff. You are supposed to be a straight line, straight A, no getting in trouble. I was just the opposite. I didn't go to class, didn't go to school, and when I was in class, I was the class clown. They always say I craved attention. So the same stuff I did then when I was younger, it's the same stuff I do now. Class clown, oh yeah, if they gave an award for that, I would have been on the honor roll.

One time I remember I put a thumbtack under the teacher's chair. Remember the silver ones, the ones that lie flat? I put one on her chair. I thought it was funny. It wasn't funny when I got that two-week suspension. I don't remember how old I was, but I remember that when my grandmom found out, oh, did I get my ass whupped. She would pin me down between her legs with my head facing down. She held my head down and whupped me. Nothing but my bare ass sticking out, and she's wearing me out with a belt. It worked, look how I turned out. I got disciplined and realized I'm not going to end up like that all the time.

Another time at church—we went to Mount Olivette Baptist Church in Overtown—when I was young, I was at Sunday school and I had a dollar and I asked the teacher for change. I needed change for a dollar or 50 cents or something, but she didn't have change. So I remember taking the scissors and cutting the dollar in half. I don't think I was trying to be funny or sarcastic. I didn't even know what being funny or sarcastic was back then. I just remember getting my ass whupped for that. When my grandma came in from church later, that Sunday school teacher told on me. "Your grandson cut this dollar in half trying to make change for a dollar." Man, I remember that. She was pissed.

Every Sunday, when I first went to church, I went to the Catholic Sunday school while my grandmother was at the Baptist church. My mom wanted me raised Catholic. After Catholic church was done, because Catholic church only lasted an hour, I would go over to see my grandma at the Baptist church. That's where I heard gospel music— I love gospel—and that's where my love of music came from. Then we'd go home and my grandma would have Sunday dinner. She was real anal about being at the table, elbows off the table, using a fork and knife for cutting. She'd be yelling at me, "Pull your pants up, tuck your shirt in." I was always dressed nice, looked neat for church. The only thing I did wrong was my gold teeth. The gold teeth I wear now come from when I was 13, saving up my allowance, saving, saving, saving. I got the top pair, and the only place I could wear them where I knew I wouldn't get caught and she couldn't see me was on the football field. That's the whole reason why I wear them now, just because it's become a part of me.

In high school, I ended up going to Miami Beach High, which is like 30 minutes away. She drove me every day and then she'd go to her teaching job. Now, did I get in trouble? Yeah, but it was never anything serious. There's no beating people up or doing foolish stuff. I'm not going to steal from somebody. I wasn't going to be getting in some gang. I just wanted to play ball. Don't be stupid. I may not have liked school, but I was just looking to have a good time. I couldn't sit in class. It was too boring. But I'm not getting into some nonsense. You read about some kid getting shot for a pair of shoes. What the heck is that? Here, have the fuckin' shoes, I don't want them. They don't mean that much.

Sometimes my grandmother would have me go live with my mother and my brother Chauncey in Los Angeles. I'd be there for a summer or whatever. During junior college, I stayed in L.A. with my mom while I was trying to get my act together with school. So I had plenty of influence from both my grandmother and my mom. My dad, nothing. And like I said, I don't care. You might. I don't.

And that's how I explain it to people when they ask why I am the way I am. You want to know why I act the way I do? Ask my mother and my grandmother. They're the ones who raised me. OK, I'm not going to turn this into some kind of Oprah show, but I'll let my grandmother do the talking.

My mother? Well, she didn't want to talk for this book. All she kept saying is, "You don't want to hear from me." Whatever that means.

Anyway, this is what my grandmother said:

BESSIE MAE FLOWERS

Chad was a good boy, but he's a jokester. He's always getting himself in trouble because he jokes all the time. Even now, now that he's in the pros, he says these things that I know the owner doesn't want to hear or have the public hear. I tell Chad all the time, you cannot say everything you want to say. He tells me, "Mommy, you don't understand."

But I do understand that I don't want him to get blackballed by the league. I ask him sometimes, "Do you know what it is to be blackballed?" He says, "Yes, Mommy, but that's not going to happen to me, you don't understand." Maybe I don't, but I worry about him and all these things he does.

It's like this year, he's not getting the ball and you just wonder: Did he say the wrong thing and now they're trying to punish him? That's why I tell him, you can't do that. The people who run the league and run the team aren't going to let you keep doing that. He says, "As long as I can still play and catch that ball, I'll be fine." I don't know.

But this is how Chad has always been. He doesn't get in big trouble, but he's mischievous. He's doing something that makes people annoyed at him. When he was in school, I'd get called all the time. "Mrs. Flowers, do you know what Chad is doing?" or "Mrs. Flowers, do you know where Chad is?" I was a teacher and I'd have to leave the school and go over there and find out what Chad was doing. As soon as I got there, he'd give me this look like, "Mommy, I'm so sorry." Well, what did you do? Did you skip class? "No, Mommy, I just had to go to the bathroom." He'd go to the bathroom and then never show up at class. He'd find something else to do.

One day when he was at Miami Beach High, he wasn't in class, so they called me. I got over there and looked around. I saw these men who were painting the walls of the school and I asked them, "Have you seen Chad Johnson?" They said, "Yes, he was painting with us for a while, he went over there." He was painting the wall! I'm thinking, what kind of nonsense is this?

So I go find him and he's sitting there talking to one of his girlfriends. As soon as he sees me, he knows. He tries to put on the charm like everything is OK, but I know better. I looked at the young lady and said, "Where are you supposed to be?" She said in class. I said, "Well, then you had best get back there." And then I started talking to Chad. "What are you doing out here? What are you doing painting the building? You're supposed to be in class."

So we'd go to the principal's office and work it out. Now, at a certain point, they just got used to punishing Chad. They did it so often it was just automatic. But they punished him one time that was really unfair. It was senior cut day. All the kids went to the beach that day and the teachers knew they were going to go. So I get a call that Chad is going to get suspended because he cut class. Well, I called right up and said, "Why are you suspending Chad because he cut? If you do that, you better suspend everybody."

I was a teacher for 42 years, so I understand how it works. I didn't put up with any silliness. If I had children who cut up in class, talked too much, I told them right away, I'm not playing with them. They got the message real fast. I couldn't teach nowadays. I'm 74 now and I'm way too short of patience. Parents just don't want to do the mothering and the fathering that they have to do. They expect the teachers to do it all, and that doesn't work. Chad wasn't like those types of kids today. Chad just took a lot longer to get the message, but I wasn't around him at school all the time.

Now, his mother and I have had our issues over the years. Like I said, I came back one day and found out she had left Chad with me and gone to Los Angeles. Chad's mother is different. She's very strong-minded, very willful. She's my daughter, and sometimes she feels like she wants to fight with me about things.

She tells me sometimes, "You stole him from me." I didn't steal Chad from her. I took care of him. That's what she wanted me to do. I even had him go live with her a lot of the time so they'd be together, but she didn't want to have him all the time. She did the best she could. She'd call and talk to him after she moved to Los Angeles. Now she's back here and she seems angry about this and that. I try to sort it out with her, but she just seems to get angrier. I don't know what to say to her.

She's my daughter from my first marriage, to Clifford Johnson. We were married and living in New York, but he was a cruel man, so I left him and came back here to Miami. Eventually I divorced him, but he helped us. He was never part of what we were trying to do. It's just like Chad's father. I see him now and again. I wish I never saw him. He never gave them a penny of help, never came by to see Chad all those years Chad was living right here, just a few blocks away.

But this is what I mean about Chad as a jokester. I think he doesn't understand that when you do it all the time, you start to wear people out. That school is an example. They were looking for a reason to do something to Chad, and even though everybody else was doing something, he got in trouble. I think that's how it could go in the NFL. They don't want all the celebrating.

Now, I don't understand that. It seems like they just want everybody to act the same, be like little robots, take all the fun out of the game. But Chad is there, pushing the celebrations and getting the NFL angry, you have to wonder when they're going to say, "Enough, Chad." That's why I keep saying to him, you're going to get blackballed. You have to be careful. He keeps saying, "Momma, you don't understand." I hope he's right, but I worry.

They fine him sometimes $10,000 for the things he does, the celebrations. If he'd just listen to me, he could save a lot of money and just give me that $10,000 and let me fix up this house. It's like that picture he took before [the 2008] season. He's on the cover of [*ESPN The Magazine*] and he's naked, except for the magazine covering up just a little. I called him and said, "Chad, why in the world did you do this?" He said, "Oh, Mommy, it was just for fun."

It's like how he jokes about me. I hear Chad tell people that I beat him and I'm thinking, "What in the world?" I ask him, "Chad, when did I ever beat you?" He doesn't really answer me. I never beat Chad. Chad was a good boy. He was mischievous and I had to come check on him a lot. But he never got in real trouble.

He went to church every Sunday. He went to the Catholic, and my husband and I would go to another church. He'd dress up in his Sunday school clothes. Sometimes he'd come back a mess from playing in the dirt or whatever, and I'd say, "Chad, what are you doing?"

And all the years of driving him around from place to place to play ball. He'd always look at me and say, "Mommy, I promise it's going to work. I'm going to make it in the NFL someday." He'd really sit there and promise. That's not why I took him. I took him because I wanted something better, something different for him. I guess he really learned, because he made it. All that driving around and making sure he was in school and talking to his teachers and counselors, it paid off for him to get to the NFL.

It took work, now, lots of work, and he didn't always listen. He took the hardheaded approach. After he got through high school, he wanted to go to all the schools in Florida, University of Florida, Miami, Florida State, and none of them would have him because of his grades. We finally got him into Langston University, and that didn't last. Langston is in Oklahoma. It's an agricultural school, and he just didn't last there. He got into too many fights and they sent him home before he ever played football.

That's when I finally had enough. I told him if he couldn't handle that, he was going to go live with his mom in Los Angeles until he figured it out. It took a while, and one day he told me, "Mommy, now I understand what you were saying to me all those years. I wish I had listened and I'd already be in the NFL."

I wish he'd listened, too.

I don't think Chad will ever remember the game when we played against each other. It was 2006 and it was in Cincinnati. In pregame, he said, "What's up? This and that, I respect your game." I said the same to him. Then we went to the game and he didn't say anything to me the whole game. . . . He was talking to Fabian Washington after almost every time Fabian was covering him. They're going back and forth, laughing and joking. Honestly, I was kind of feeling left out. I kid you not.

—**Nnamdi Asomugha,** Oakland Raiders Pro Bowl cornerback

SIX

TALKING TRASH

SOME PEOPLE ROLL THEIR eyes when I say that everybody in the NFL likes me. They think that I talk so much trash that everybody wants to knock my head off. I'm sure there's a couple of guys out there like that, but really everybody else loves how I'm talking trash. I'm making it fun.

That's what fans don't understand. But I'll have Ronde Barber and Brian Dawkins explain it. Ronde has played 12 years with Tampa Bay and Brian has played 13 years with Philadelphia. They're both Pro Bowlers, so they know what's up.

Barber: "It's not as much trash talk as it is a running conversation. He'll talk to you about what's going on in his life. He's talking about something completely outside of the game. Honestly, I think it's a distraction method. It's less about football and more about everything else. But really, he comes off like a good dude. His antics get in the way of what kind of person he really is.

"Chad is misunderstood, but I think he likes being misunderstood. The public persona is more of a selling point. I think he's a great guy. You have one image of him, and then you play against him and that image completely changes."

Dawkins: "You expect Chad to talk, and he's talking about stuff that has nothing to do with the game. He's all in left field talking about whatever. It has nothing to do with the next play or what has happened in the game up to that point. Nothing. During the game, it's anything that comes into his head. *Anything.* And, like I said, if you get into that, he'll take you out of your game. If you get to the sideline and say, 'Man, Chad is talking about something that has nothing to do with the game,' then he's got you out of your game. You're out of where you're supposed to be.

"Fans misunderstand it because they take it too seriously. It's not that we, as players, don't take him seriously. You have to because he's one of the best receivers in the game. But you can't sell the farm on what he does by talking. You can't say that his talking is all that he's about, because that's not it. He's playing with you while he's trying to beat you. He's smart that way, if you let him do it."

Like I said, the other guys in the league get it. They understand. It's the serious fans who don't understand me, that think I'm just this guy trying to tell everybody how great I am.

Well, I am great, but that goes without saying.

When I'm looking across the line at a cornerback who is afraid of me, not ready to play, this is like having sex with somebody new. It's like, "Man, I'm going to get me some of that!" But then it's like, it gets boring. That's why I always want the cornerback, that other guy on the other side of me, to be ready. That's why I'm talking so much trash.

It's like the first time I played against Cortland Finnegan of Tennessee. I didn't know who he was at the time. He was a seventh-round pick out of nowhere, but now I know he's good. Real good. Made the Pro Bowl. He's quick as hell, feisty little shit, too. I like him 'cause he's not afraid to talk back, either. That's why he came down to Miami to work out with me this off-season. Good dude.

But the first time he covered me, he remembers this to this day, he comes up to press me. He's trying to get his hands on me and stop me from getting into my route right away. Guys try that because they don't think I'll be physical, but what they don't understand is that I can get right around them so fast. Then, when they start really reaching, I can swipe them away, no problem.

Anyway, Finnegan comes up to the line, and I look at him and say, "You probably don't want to do that, I'm the best you ever seen." Hey, I want to see what he's about. Cortland said he kind of chuckled when I said that right in the middle of a play, but that's what it's all about. I'm trying to have fun and get these guys going.

HUE JACKSON

former Cincinnati Bengals wide receivers coach

Don't let Chad fool you with that "Everybody loves me, even when I trash talk stuff." Not everybody is so into that. Now, I'm not saying I think he should stop. Chad needs to be Chad. He has to be hyped and he has to believe that the guy on the other side is competing as hard

as he can. There's no question about that. That's his game. That's
what he's about.

And that stuff doesn't bother me. Hey, I talked when I played.
That's part of the fun. And if you talk, I want you to keep talking. I
don't want you to get scared and back down from what you are. This
is a game where you have to be on top of your stuff. You have to go
in there with courage and be ready. I don't want some guy who's going
to cower when we get into a game. Say what you mean and back it up.
If you don't talk, that's fine. That's great. If you talk, don't back down.

But Chad can get on some other guys' nerves, and I saw it plenty
of times. When I was there, before I went to Baltimore, and we played
the Ravens, Chad would get on Chris McAlister's nerves all the time.
Chris literally wanted to fight him. Chris is a strong corner, kind of
guy who wants to play physical because he's pretty big, pretty stout
[McAlister is a bigger cornerback by NFL standards, at 6-1, 206]. So
he's always trying to bump Chad, but Chad can make him miss with
his moves and then Chad starts talking even more. After a while,
Chris is just pissed off, fuming mad.

This one time in a game, I swear, Chris took a swing at Chad right
at the line of scrimmage, missed, and then was chasing Chad all over
the field as Chad ran his route, still swinging at him trying to knock
him out. That was funny. But there wasn't any love going on right then.

When I'm talking trash to other players, I never stop. Not for one
minute. I'm going the whole game. I'm starting in pregame. They have
this rule where you're not supposed to go over to the other side of the
field where the other team is warming up before a game. I always go like

two steps over that line, just far enough that I know I won't get called. The ref will just come over and say, "Chad, you got to get back over." But I'm gettin' as close as I can to talk some shit to the other team, so they can hear me.

I'm talking the whole time, no rest, none. Like I said, I gotta be that way because I want that other guy on the other side of me at the top of his game. If he's at the top of his game, I have to be at the top of mine. When you talk trash to somebody, you have to do your research. I make sure I know where a guy went to high school, college, where he grew up, every detail I can find.

When I come to the line and say, "Yo, this ain't Lincoln High no more," guys get a little distracted. I never get personal. Nothing about your mom or wife, nothing like that. I don't have to get into that to talk trash. Most guys try to ignore me, but I get to them eventually, especially if they're young guys. They try to talk back, but I just keep coming and coming and coming, wear them down something serious. They just can't keep up, and if the guys on the other sideline start hearing it, sometimes I get them laughing at their own guy. That's hilarious. Ray Lewis compared it to Muhammad Ali.

RAY LEWIS
Baltimore Ravens Pro Bowl linebacker

It's nonstop with Chad and it's fun. It's the greatest competition you can ever get, 'cause he's telling you, "I'm willing to tell you that my skill is better than yours." That's all he does, and that's what makes Chad Chad. I told him one time . . . one of the most classic lines that

I've ever heard a player say on a football field was when we were playing in Cincinnati and he looked at our cornerback, Chris McAlister,
and said, "Come here, come right here." It's right in the middle of a
play, the ball is about to be snapped, and Chad is saying to Chris,
"Come here." You don't get that from anybody else. Nobody else. If
you do, they might do it quietly. But Chad, he don't say nothing quietly.
It's the way it should be done, all the time. And if he don't do it that
way, it's going to deter from who he is.

It's not ugly. It's competition. It's the same thing I do when I'm in
the trenches, whether I'm talking to a quarterback or talking to a running back. It's the same thing . . . Chad is confident in his ability when
he gets on a football field. Why wouldn't you talk about it? It's like
Muhammad Ali. He was the greatest of all time, and every time he
went in the ring, he told people what he was going to do. He didn't win
them all, but the bottom line was that some people liked him and
some people didn't, but you have to keep going.

Ray is so right about Ali. Ali was the first great trash talker, and it
changed the world. Look at what Ali influenced. Rap music, hip-hop,
got people thinking in bigger ways. For athletes, he made guys realize
that you have to promote yourself in a big way, don't expect everybody
else to do it for you. But you better back it up, and that's what Ali did.
He put on a show for everybody and he was great. He was one of a kind.

Ray is a good talker, but me and him don't really go at it because he's
not in the secondary, and he just laughs at me. Among the defensive
backs, there are a couple of guys who can talk with me pretty good. Cornerback DeAngelo Hall and cornerback Fred Smoot, who are both with

Washington now. DeAngelo used to be in Atlanta. The league should mike me up with those guys every week. That would be amazing, hilarious. I would die to have them on my schedule every year. I'd give anything. I promise you. If they could mike us up in a game for four quarters, people would pay just to hear that.

One guy who gets rattled every time we play is New York Jets linebacker Bart Scott, who used to be in Baltimore. Yeah, he cusses me out, tells me to get the fuck out of the huddle, the whole nine yards. He tells the whole defense not to talk to me because I'm trying to get in their heads. He hates when I talk to them. The funny part is I'm getting in his head and he doesn't even realize it. He's talking, but not the way I am. I'm there for a reason, I have a motive when I talk. Most of the guys on their team just ignore me like Ray. I talk to [Baltimore Pro Bowl safety] Ed Reed and he just says, "Go on, Chad." They all don't pay me any attention. Bart is the only one I can get a rise out of. I'm smiling ear to ear and he is dead serious. Pittsburgh players don't pay me any attention, but they all talk shit, every last one of them, except Troy Polamalu.

Troy is real religious, real serious on the field. Good guy, great player. He does some stuff that drives some offensive guys crazy. Like right before the snap, he'll turn his back on the play. Completely turn around and look back at the other safety, some shit like that, and then turn around again just before the ball snaps. Kind of freaky. And he guesses on routes all the time, jumps on stuff, gambles. He's great on that.

And Troy gets the trash-talking stuff by me. Actually, he was pretty funny talking about it. Troy said, "Chad is never like, 'I'm going to eat your kids.' I've never met anybody like that really. Well, maybe actually Joey [Porter]. Actually, our team is like that."

Like I said, I have to talk shit. It keeps me at the top of my game. I'm trying to force myself to continue to play at a high level. But most fans just don't understand what it's all about. Trash talking is fun. Some people get all serious and think that's not acceptable or that I'm mocking the opponent. That's not it at all. It's about staying hyped and having a good time.

I'm just clowning with guys, like the time in 2004 where I was joking with Joey Porter when he was playing for Pittsburgh. Like I said before, Joey is intense. He's always trying to look all mean and tough, like he's going to bite somebody's head off. Now, he might actually do that, so you gotta be careful, but I'm always clowning on Joey.

Anyway, the week before we play Pittsburgh that season, J. P. and William Green, this running back Cleveland took in the first round one year, get into a fight and get kicked out.

Before the game even starts!

Now, think about that, we're just talking about walking around during warm-ups and my man J. P. is getting so out of control he's fighting *before the game starts.* Like, Joey, come on, chill the fuck out.

So we play the Steelers the next week after that and here's my chance. We're in Cincinnati, on my turf, so it's all cool. The fans don't even really notice. I walk up to Joey before the game and start shouting at him, "Come on, let's just go to the middle of the field and fight. Right now, man, right here. Middle of the field, let's go." Joey is waving at me, telling me to get the heck outta there. I got him all annoyed, but he's smiling a little. All the other guys on the Steelers are laughing. Pittsburgh linebacker James Farrior is just laughing the whole time.

I love getting on J. P., 'cause he's so intense. He's got his shirt all rolled up before the game, showing off his abs and trying to intimidate people. I walk up to him, roll up my shirt, and show off my physique, like I'm going to be scaring those dudes. That's funny.

It's like Joey said: "Chad just always wants to play with me before the game, take me out of my serious mode that I be in. So if I'm arguing with somebody else, he'll come over that and start acting funny and start playing with me. He's trying to have fun with me. I'm trying to focus and be mad before the game, and he's joking. I'm like, 'Man, get away from me.' He likes to pick at you to get you to say something."

Farrior was funny, too. He said I was like everybody's "little brother, just annoying us until we get all frustrated with him." I'll take that, even if I'm the older brother in my family.

And it's not just because I'm black that I talk. The white guys in the league love to talk trash, too. Jared Allen from Minnesota [he used to be in Kansas City], he loves what I do and he likes to talk a little. Everybody is into it. It's like the stories they tell about Larry Bird when he was playing in the NBA. He was one of the best trash talkers in the league. He did it kind of quiet, so people didn't notice as much, but he was confident.

Does talking trash make people want to hit me harder? Come on, you don't think guys in this league don't already want to hit you hard? That's the point of playing in the NFL. You don't get here as a defensive guy if you don't hit hard.

It's my job to make sure they don't hit me, and sometimes, if you get the other guys revved up too much, that can work to your advantage.

They want to hit you so hard that they come too fast, I can make a move, and they miss me. Instead of just making a tackle and getting me down on the ground, I'm running past them because they want to knock me out of the game.

You see, I got it figured out in my head. I know what guys are trying to do. It's like Farrior, who was saying I'm like everybody's little brother, annoying everybody. He knows what I'm trying to do: "It's tough to get a good lick on Chad. He's a smart guy, he knows all the tricks about how to get down when somebody is about to get him. I don't think I ever got a clean shot on him, but I wish."

Some guys try to make fun of me, say I'm not tough enough to take a hit from them. Whatever, I ain't stupid, either. I'm strong, but I'm also skinny. I'm not getting in there and blocking real hard or taking some big shot. I'll do what I can, shield guys for the running back, but what good is it for me to start throwing my body around with all those guys who are bigger than me?

You know what's going to happen? I'm going to get hurt, and then I can't play and then I can't help our team win. That's what it's going to be, and then what does that do for everybody? Nothing.

I heard Plaxico Burress wrote in his book that he called it a "business decision." I like that. That's a smart way of putting it. You gotta know how to avoid those big collisions so that you can keep playing.

But you also got to get defensive guys trying to do stuff like that. You gotta get in their head, try to get them going. Get them playing too hard or not hard enough. Like I said, I want guys playing hard because it brings out the best in me. But if I can get a guy distracted a little bit, out of his game, all the better.

I'm just not going to get all cheap about it. Like I said, it's none of that "Your momma" stuff. At least not serious. It's all going to be fun. It's going to be all over the place.

Oh yeah, Nnamdi, sorry you felt left out. I won't do that again. I promise.

Covering Chad Johnson is like ridiculous. He's so smooth with his routes and it's impossible to get a good read on him. Me, I like to be feisty with receivers, get in their head and bother them all the time. You can't do that with Chad, because you can't get your hands on him to slow down his routes, and you can't get in his head because he never stops talking long enough to let you say anything.

—**Cortland Finnegan,** Tennessee Titans
Pro Bowl cornerback

SEVEN

WHY MY BEST GAME REALLY SUCKED

THIS IS WHAT IT'S like to have a defensive back completely fried, just torched. I was running at San Diego safety Marlon McCree on an angle from the right side of the field on what looked like a post route. McCree was completely by himself, with no help to either side.

And no hope.

Now, this wasn't the greatest pass route I ever ran or my best catch. Frankly, I really don't remember most of my plays or my games. That's not what it's about. I'm looking ahead. I'm thinking about what I'm going to do next, not what I did in the past. That's why when all my boys from back home talk about all the great games we had way back when, I really don't remember.

I'm living for the moment. I'm trying to have fun right now, all the time, especially when I'm on the field.

But this play in the game against San Diego is pretty amazing. It was part of my best game ever and part of two weeks when I set NFL history. Over two games, no receiver ever did what I did. Not Jerry Rice, not Marvin Harrison, not Cris Carter. Nobody. Against San Diego and New Orleans in consecutive weeks in 2006, I had 17 catches for 450 yards and five touchdowns total. I had 11 catches for 260 yards and two scores against the Chargers, one of the biggest games in NFL history. Then I had six more catches for 190 and three touchdowns against New Orleans. I was unreal. Our quarterback, Carson Palmer, was unreal. We were so much on the same page, it was sick.

Carson could have thrown the ball with his eyes closed on some plays and I still would have caught it, that's how on-target we were. And this play against the Chargers and Marlon McCree was the perfect example.

First of all, you can't blame this on McCree. We caught them in the exact right defense in the exact right situation.

I'll go through the situation first. We were up 14–0 already in the first quarter. Carson is smokin' already. He's seven-for-seven for 112 yards before we even run this play. He's completed passes to four different guys, including three to T. J. Houshmandzadeh and two to me. The Chargers have no fuckin' clue how to stop us. None.

Worse, the Chargers' offense is starting slow and their punter kicks two shitty punts on their first two possessions. On their third possession, it gets really bad for them. They're facing a third-and-11 and their quarterback, Philip Rivers, hits Keenan McCardell for 31 yards. But then they lose the play when it gets reversed on a replay and they have to punt from their own 8-yard line.

We end up getting the ball at our own 49-yard line. We're basically at midfield, we're hot, and we're ready to bury them. You don't get a lot of chances like this in the NFL. Maybe once or twice a season (make that once for us). So this is when we're ready to deliver what should be the kill shot, put the game away, take a chance on a big play to really kick their ass.

It was perfect. San Diego was playing what's called a "quarters" coverage, something like a two-deep where both the safeties are in the middle of the field. The key difference is that in quarters, the safety is all by himself in certain situations because the cornerbacks don't drop deep if you run the right play.

This is what I'm saying. I'm on the outside right of the formation. I'm standing just outside the numbers on the field, T. J. is in the slot next to me, and the Chargers don't bring their other corner to the other side. They didn't change the coverage at all. So as we're lining up and Carson is making the snap count, I can see what's about to happen and I'm waving my arm.

Now, when I'm waving my arm, that used to be a signal to our old wide receivers coach and Carson that I was going to change up the route. But that's not what I was trying to do here. I'm telling them both, I'm open, this shit is a touchdown. Let that fuckin' ball fly.

We snap it and it sets up perfectly. I start to run a post and T. J. runs a shallow out pattern so that cornerback Quentin Jammer on that side has to cover me. It opens up like, well, you know what I'm saying. Like I said before, I'm thinking I'm going to get me some of that. By the time I get into the deep part of the secondary, it's just me and McCree and I basically have my choice of what to do and he knows it. I can run the post or I can go to the corner. He has to guess.

I run as hard as I can right at him, plant my left foot in the ground as hard as I can to sell him on the post route. Then I break back to the right toward the corner of the field and McCree spins like a top. This is a post-corner route. Usually, you have two guys to beat on this route. When you have only one, it's over.

Carson lets it fly and I run under it. McCree is 20 yards from me by the time I catch the ball. It was so easy that it was ridiculous. It's beautiful. Best part, we're up 21–0 and the Chargers are reeling.

At least I thought they were.

Here's what sucks about this game. I go off for 260 yards and it's not enough. The kick in the ass about this game is that we lose. Yeah, we're up 21–0 and I'm just getting started and we still lost this game 49–41. It's our third loss in a row and fifth in six games and leaves us 4–5 after we went 11–5 the year before and made the playoffs. We end up 8–8 that season and miss the playoffs, and that game hurt a lot. We had this under control and we'd already lost three games by six points or less, one of those by two points and another by one. Brutal, just brutal.

The other thing is that San Diego was good that season. They were already 6–2 and rolling pretty good. By the end of the season, we found out just how good they were. They finished 14–2, best record in the league. LaDainian Tomlinson was unbelievable, set the NFL record for touchdowns and won the MVP. They should have won the title, but they fucked up a playoff game against New England. Funny part is that Marlon McCree was one of the main guys who screwed up that playoff game when he fumbled after grabbing an interception.

Anyway, think about that. We had the Chargers on the ropes. We had the best team in the league totally on the ropes. We were killing them, and by the fourth quarter, the Chargers are in control so much that they end kneeling down on the ball for the last possession and I'm sick to my stomach.

What can I say? We did the same shit the next year against Cleveland in 2007. Everybody remembers that game, not because I had 11 catches for 209 yards and two touchdowns, but because we lost 51–45. What does everybody remember about that game? They see Braylon Edwards making a diving catch, getting up, and going into the end zone. That's what I mean about winning, that's what people remember. That's where everything starts. Same thing happened in 2005, the year we make the playoffs. We host Indianapolis at home, I go off for eight catches, 189 yards and a touchdown, we lose 45–37, and everybody talks about how Peyton Manning, Marvin Harrison, and Reggie Wayne are the best passing combination in the NFL.

I remember saying after that game against Cleveland in 2007, "Hey, it's not the defense's fault. If the other team scores 51, we have to score 52." And I'm the bad guy on the team?

Anyway, back to the San Diego game. Like I said, we're up 21–0 and everything is rolling. Carson completes another pass to me for 13 yards on the next drive and now he's nine-for-nine for 176 yards. I'm pumped for Carson, because this was the season that he came back from the knee injury against Pittsburgh in the playoffs nine months before. The fact that he made it back for the start of the season was awesome, but then he's taking shit from the media because they think he has happy feet and is scared of the rush. It's ridiculous crap, but I know he was pissed about it. It just took him a while to get back in the groove, because we couldn't throw as much in the off-season.

Finally, Carson throws an incomplete and, sure as shit, it's on a throw to me. The funny part is, that's the only incomplete he threw to me all day. Think about that. He throws my way 12 times and we complete 11. That's way harder than shooting three-pointers. That's ridiculous. We were stupid good that day.

Anyway, we're driving again and get in position for a 51-yard field goal, but our kicker, Shayne Graham, misses. Shayne is a good kicker— I actually feel bad for him because he got franchised by the Bengals this year when he thought he was going to be able to leave the team. But 51 yards ain't easy. Shit happens.

The Chargers start to get their offense going and they score a touchdown to make it 21–7, but we're still rolling. We go right back down the field. Carson is totally on fire still. He completes 11 of 12 passes. Hits me three more times, so I have eight catches for 117 yards in the first half. That's pretty awesome, but nothing so out of control that I'm thinking about any records or anything. We're just moving the ball and we're doing it great. We start the drive with 5:27 remaining, and Carson runs the drive so perfect that we score another touchdown with 21 seconds left to make it 28–7.

This is the shit we should be doing all the time. We can do this to anybody. The thing is that this is what we're capable of and we can't seem to keep it together in Cincinnati. That's why I'm so frustrated, why I said the things I said after the 2007 season. I see what we can be. I see what we could do if management would be behind us and make the right moves. It's like I said before the 2008 season, when I was being interviewed by Stephen A. Smith of ESPN. What I said—and I've always said—is that I love Cincinnati and I love my teammates. But I'm tired of hearing the same old speech from the coaches and management at the beginning of training camp about how we're working toward getting to the big game at the end of the season when that's not getting backed up by the powers that be.

Anyway, I know I'm on a fuckin' rant, but it's upsetting and this game is exactly what I'm talking about. We're dominating in the first half. Carson is 20 of 23 for 282 yards. He was so hot, I was afraid to touch him. I thought I'd get burned. This game should be over. Completely over, fuckin' done. We even keep rolling on offense, but we can't stop the Chargers from coming back.

We go three-and-out the first two times we get the ball in the second half. What makes it worse is we get called for silly penalties, like tripping and holding, and all of a sudden San Diego gets the ball and goes right at us. They're in a hurry-up, shotgun offense the whole time on their first drive and score in like two minutes. Now it's 28–14. The next time they get the ball, they do to us what we did to them in the first half. They get the momentum and, boom, complete a 46-yard touchdown pass. It gets worse, because on that play, our starting cornerback, Deltha O'Neal, gets hurt and has to be helped into the locker room.

Now it's 28–21 and I'm like, shit, we got a game going. But that's cool, just get Ochocinco the ball and we'll be cool. That's exactly what we do. Carson hits me over the middle for 35 yards and now we're at the San Diego 22. Seriously, the Chargers have no clue how to cover me in this game. None. I'm at 152 yards and we still have a quarter and a half to play.

It didn't matter what San Diego did. Man, zone, two-deep, whatever, we had an answer. We get down to the 4-yard line on the next play and it's like, "Cool, we're back under control, just score the touchdown and we're back up by 14." But we stall and only get a field goal. That sucks. Now we're up 31–21, and even though we got the lead, it's still tense.

And for good reason. San Diego gets the ball and scores in like three minutes to make it 31–28.

Hey, but never fear, Ocho is here. We get the ball, and in one play we got a 10-point lead again and I've got the biggest game of my career. I line up on the left against Drayton Florence. The Chargers didn't switch their corners, because they had confidence in Florence, almost as much as Jammer, at the time. But I roast his ass and the safety, Terrence Kiel, never comes over to help. I go 74 yards for the touchdown and we're up 38–28 with like three minutes left in the third quarter.

Again, I really didn't know all of this until my receiver coach, Hue Jackson, came up to me and said, "Man, you got over 200 yards. You're getting close to an NFL record." I really didn't know. I mean, I know it was a good game, but I'm not doing that where I keep track of every yard I have or anything like that. What's the use? I know I'm going to get my yards and my plays.

But the way Hue talks about it, I'm in a total zone:

HUE JACKSON

former Cincinnati Bengals wide receivers coach

He was in one of those states where everything was right. There were no off-field issues, no on-field issues, nothing. Things were just right. He knew he was going to be a big part of the game plan because we made sure he understood that during practice that week. When great athletes know that, when you create that environment in practice where they know they are going to be a big part of the game plan, you can see a change in how they approach the game.

The stars were all aligned for Chad for that week and the next couple. He was good, he knew what we were going to do. He trusted that. Most importantly, we didn't overthink it. To me, you keep working your best players. You feed them the ball. Now, as coaches, sometimes we screw that up. We start to think, "Hey, the other team knows we're going to do this, so we need to adjust and do that." To me, you ride your best guys until the other team figures out a way to stop them. You pay a guy big money, you get your money's worth. In that San Diego game, they couldn't figure out a way to stop Chad and we didn't stop giving it to him. It's like I say, runners want to run, piano players want to play, receivers want to catch the ball. When a guy is catching it like that, you just keep going to him.

The other thing is that the more he gets the ball like that, the better he plays in everything. He did it all in that game. He caught, he ran after the catch, he blocked, every little thing we asked. . . . And he's telling the truth about the stats. He didn't know. He was just totally into the game. For me, I keep track of stuff like that because I want to make sure I know what's going on in the game, that we're getting the ball to guys. I saw it flash up on the scoreboard that he had like 200-something yards, and I went over and said, "Buddy, you're close to an NFL record."

The record is 336 yards by Willie "Flipper" Anderson back in 1989, so I'm on pace to break that. Again, I don't really care. I'm into the game.

So what happens? San Diego scores in like nothing flat. They drive to our 2-yard line by the last play of the third quarter. On the first play of the fourth quarter, Tomlinson scores his third touchdown of the game. And I think I'm having a big day. Now it's back to a three-point game, 38–35, and our offense is back out on the field, feeling like we gotta keep rolling. San Diego has scored five straight touchdowns the last five drives they've had.

Of course, we make the one big mistake of the game for us. We run a deep drop with Carson to set up a big play, but the play breaks down. Before Carson can get rid of it, San Diego linebacker Shaun Phillips sacks him, Carson fumbles, and the Chargers have the ball at our 9-yard line. They score on the next play when Tomlinson scores his fourth touchdown. Four touchdowns.

Tomlinson was so good that season, it was like he's not even running. He set the NFL record with 28 rushing touchdowns that season and caught three more touchdowns. That's 31 touchdowns in one season. It wasn't even the first time he scored four touchdowns that season. He did it like four weeks before that against San Francisco.

But you want to know what makes Tomlinson so great? He can cut on his inside leg when he's running. Most people don't understand what that means, so let me explain. When you're to the left or the right side of the field, 99 percent of players have to plant their outside leg to cut. If you're running left, you plant your left leg. If you're going right, you plant your right leg. It's pretty simple. You can pretty much figure it out just walking around.

If you try to plant on your inside leg, it's totally unnatural because your weight is going the other direction and you can't stop your body.

That's how it's supposed to work for just about everybody. The other thing is that your inside leg is usually bent, so it doesn't support your weight as easily.

This is where Tomlinson is a freak. He can cut on his inside or his outside leg. That way, defenders can't get a read on him at all. Just watch when he runs outside and starts to get to full speed. It looks almost like he's faking with his shoulders as he makes the defender miss. It's awesome to watch.

I do something similar when I run routes, but we'll get into that later in the book.

Anyway, Tomlinson has four touchdowns and now we're down 42–38. Like, what happened? Fortunately, there's almost the entire fourth quarter to play, but now we're losing and the Chargers are acting like they're trying to blow us out in our own place.

We get the ball back, and the first play, they give me the ball again. But this time it's on a double reverse. We hardly ever run this play and I get stuck for no gain. It's the only time San Diego stops me all game. Then we run, run, run, run, get to midfield, miss a couple of throws, and have to punt it away. Finally, our defense holds them to a three-and-out, and then we get the ball and score a field goal. It's 42–41 with about eight minutes left in the game.

San Diego then proceeds to stick the knife in our back and just twist away. Our defense gets them into third-down situations four times on the next drive. Four straight third downs and the Chargers convert them all. The last one is a short touchdown pass, and now it's 49–41 with 2:29 left in the game.

How the fuck did this happen? We've gone from being in control, to the game being close, to now needing a miracle. We need a touchdown and a two-point conversion just to go to overtime. Are you kidding me?

But OK, we gotta do whatever it takes. No room for bitching now. We get the ball at the 40-yard line. Carson hits Chris Henry for 11 and then comes back to me for 22 and 12. We're at the San Diego 15 just like that with 1:09 to play. It's perfect. We got at least four shots to tie this, if not more.

That's all we get. Carson throws incomplete to Tony Stewart, incomplete to Henry, gets no gain on a check down to Kenny Watson, and then an incomplete to Glenn Holt, some backup receiver and kick returner.

I've got 11 catches, 260 yards, and two touchdowns, but what does it mean? Whoop-di-fucking-doo, that's what it means. I watch the Chargers kneel down for two straight plays in our own stadium after we were kicking their ass. That's what frustrating is all about.

If there's one good thing about this game it's that the coaches realize the passing game is back. All that shit about Carson having problems gets blown out of the water and the offensive coaches are thinking—like the players are thinking again—we can do anything we want. The defensive coaches were probably freaked out, but all I can do is control my part. I want those guys to do well. Get us the ball as much as they can, but I don't know shit about what they do.

Anyway, we get to New Orleans, and on the first series I'm still hot as hell from the last game. Let my man Hue Jackson tell you about my first touchdown:

HUE JACKSON
former Cincinnati Bengals wide receivers coach

In 2004, 2005, and 2006, there wasn't anybody in the NFL who was better at wide receiver than Chad. Nobody. People who criticize him say, "Oh, but he didn't have the touchdowns." He had 25 touchdowns over those three years. But that's because when we got into the red zone, we'd get away from him. We had T. J., and he's one of the best at reading coverages in the red zone. That's what he does well. Plus, the other team knows that they have to take away Chad at that point. They don't have a choice. So, as you get closer, his opportunities get smaller and smaller.

But in the middle of the field nobody can handle Chad, and this first touchdown against the Saints was amazing. Carson Palmer would tell you, if Chad is one-on-one, don't even think about throwing to anybody else, just throw it to him. On this play, he's on the left and we run an eight route and the cornerback has pretty good coverage. He's in position to knock this down or even intercept it if he cuts under it. Carson throws it on a line and the corner starts to jump it and I'm thinking, "Oh, shit." But Chad just snags it away and goes the rest of the way for the touchdown.

That one was 41 yards, so in one game and one series, I have 301 yards. Damn, this is sweet, and at least we're winning 7–0. The rest of the first half is back and forth. We were a little worried, because New Orleans wants to throw the ball so much with Drew Brees. Fortunately, we intercept him twice, but we end up running the ball a lot to kill the clock and keep our defense off the field, and we end up with a 10–7 lead at halftime.

Nothing happens in the third quarter and New Orleans finally ties it at 10–10 to start the fourth quarter. We get the ball back and we're working the running game some more and we're getting the Saints to cheat up against us finally. We're patient, and we get to a third-and-2 situation and the Saints are thinking the ball is going to T. J. on this play. The safeties are collapsing on him, and I run over the top of the defense, Carson lays it out perfectly for a 60-yard touchdown, and we have the lead at 17–10.

Our defense holds New Orleans to a three-and-out and back out we come. Rudi Johnson breaks a 22-yard run to get to about midfield and then Carson hits me again for 48 yards to get to the Saints' 4-yard line. I get the next pass for the touchdown and we're up 24–10 midway through the fourth quarter.

This time, we get the kill shot. Our defense intercepts Brees one more time and returns it for a touchdown, we end up winning 31–16, and I finish with six catches for 190 yards. I stay pretty hot the next three games. I average over 100 yards a game and we get a four-game winning streak going. We almost get to the point where we can forget about that loss to San Diego, then we lose the last three and end up out of the playoffs.

I've had some pretty huge games. But those two games, back-to-back, that's as on fire as I have been. Everything was right there. I was so confident in everything I did. It was like the time that I turned to a teammate on the sideline and said, "If they stop me today with any coverage—two-man, 55, man-to-man, cover 2—I will give you my game check."

And people tell me all the time about the favorite catch I've made that they remember. I think the funniest was this 51-yarder I had against Baltimore in 2004. It was late in the season and I went down the right sideline. I took the ball right off of Chris McAlister's helmet. Pissed him off big-time. It was at Baltimore and we won 27–26. I didn't score. I fell down after the catch at like the 8-yard line and then got to the 4 before the Baltimore safety tackled me.

At the time, Hue Jackson was giving me shit all the time about how I wasn't running after the catch very much. So I got up after I got tackled and dove into the end zone. I ran back to the sideline and said to Hue, "What'd you think of that?" I'm smiling and laughing, and he looks at me and says, "You're a fool." He loved it. He loved that catch.

And best of all, we won.

The celebrations? I love them, honestly. I don't have a particular favorite, but that part of the game is kind of disappearing, the entertainment value of it. But Chad won't let it go quietly. The Hall of Fame jacket? Yeah, I know some guys were upset, but I thought it was pretty cool.

—**Ronde Barber,** Tampa Bay Buccaneers
Pro Bowl cornerback

EIGHT

CELEBRATIONS

I DON'T UNDERSTAND THIS whole deal in the NFL about celebrations. The league is always finding some way to ban something I'm doing or something somebody wants to do. It's like the end of the Super Bowl this year, what's the big story about? Should Santonio Holmes have been flagged for celebrating after he caught the game-winning touchdown—you know, when he did that LeBron James thing and threw the ball in the air?

I mean, really, are you serious? We're worried about that after this dude has just made one of the greatest catches in Super Bowl history? He's living every player's dream and we're worried about how he celebrates? Come on, man, this is getting ridiculous. But that's what it's all about. People think we're supposed to be like robots, just hand the ball back to the ref and go back to the sideline, maybe high-five somebody.

Look, some guys want to play that way. They want to keep themselves under control so they don't lose it. Fine, whatever. Not me. That's not what I'm here for. As I said one time in an interview I did with ESPN: "People tell me I got to tone it down. Man, you know what I been through to get here and you want me to stop having fun? Man, it's not happening."

The league comes up with a rule for everything we try to do, but they don't get it. What are the fans there for? It ain't like they're going to the opera and just politely clapping. They're there to get hyped, get jacked, get excited. They want to see big plays, they want to be on the edge of their seats. They want to be clapping and dancing themselves. The fans LOVE the celebrations.

How do I know? They tell me, for one thing. Hell, my coaches even love them. Ask Bob Bratkowski, the offensive coordinator with the Bengals. He tells me all the time to calm it down, but I know what he thinks. Here's what Brat really thinks:

"I would never let Chad see me chuckle at his celebrations, but I chuckle sometimes. Chad is clever. He's funny. I tell him all the time, I wish you'd spend as much time watching film as you do thinking about what you're going to do next when you score."

Or just go on YouTube and check it out. Right there, you'll find all my celebrations, the Best of Ochocinco, right there. Man, I should do a special video and just sell it, but the NFL would probably want a cut. And that's the messed-up thing. The NFL has it two ways. They fine you if you celebrate, but then they use the highlights of our celebrations to promote the games.

You think I'm lying, you're dead wrong. Ask Joey Porter, the Pro

Bowl linebacker from Miami who used to play in Pittsburgh. Joey goes to the Pro Bowl one year, they score a big touchdown, and all of a sudden he gets flagged for it. Then guess what the league does?

I'll have J. P. explain it to you: "The league doesn't look at [celebrating] the same way as us. They think if we're having fun, trying to market ourselves, that's bad. But what's bad about that? The whole thing is that if the league can't get a piece of it, they don't want you to do it. They so greedy, they want it all. They don't want you to do nothing that helps you. But if it helps them, OK. One time, we got a flag for celebrating in the Pro Bowl and they fined us. Then they used that same clip of us celebrating to promote the Pro Bowl. It was the 2003 Pro Bowl. [Cornerback] Ty Law got an interception for a touchdown and we all ran down in the end zone, dancing with him. They flag us and fine us, but then the next year, that's a highlight of the Pro Bowl. They use that for the commercial to promote the game. How is something that you say is bad and you fine us, but then you use it for yourself? I don't understand that. Whose advantage is that for?"

The man has a point. Or here's another way of looking at it: ESPN is the biggest thing in sports programming, right? They know what's fun, what sells, right? So they do a commercial with me a couple of years ago about celebrations. Come on, right there, what does that tell you? That tells you that they know what draws the fans, what the fans like.

That commercial was funny, and we cut it up a couple of ways. First, you got Stuart Scott, who gets up and does a corny dance and says, "Little old-school, pop and lock and boo-ya." I laugh real quick and say, "Boo-no." Then Steve Levy jumps onto the table and starts shaking, saying, "Sizzling, bacon, action." I give him credit, that took some guts to do that. But I get a great line: "Are you serious? If I did that in public, I'd fine myself."

Anyway, it's a great commercial and the thing it really tells you is about celebrations, what everybody thinks of them. ESPN even did a top 10 celebrations after the 2006 season when the NFL was putting in all these new rules banning celebrations. Now, all 10 should have been me, but I understand they have to represent some of the other players in the league. Give it a little balance. Anyway, I had three of the top five celebrations.

I was at No. 5 with my sign that said, "Dear NFL, Please Don't Fine Me Again." That wasn't bad. I liked that one OK. Then I was No. 4 with me putting the ball with the pylon against Baltimore and then doing the Tiger Woods fist pump. I liked that one a lot. That was pretty creative. Then I was at No. 3 when I proposed to the cheerleader during the Bengals–Colts game in 2005. That was after Terrell Owens grabbed the pom-poms from the cheerleaders during a game, so I just went to the next level and then I wrote on the marking board, "T. O. I got you baby."

See, me and T. O. and Steve Smith, we took celebrations to a whole new level in 2005. I mean, that stuff was outrageous, awesome stuff. Steve did the rowboat against Minnesota after they had the Loveboat scandal earlier in the year. Very funny. And another thing about that game: Steve had 201 yards on 11 catches, and that was on a 69-yard touchdown while they were kicking Minnesota's ass. It's not like he did it in some close game where he could have cost the team a big penalty or something. It was just for fun, let the fans have a good time. Anyway, Steve had another one that was great after one of his kids was born.

Steve acted like he was wiping the baby's butt, you know, a little tribute to just having had a kid. When he scored, he laid the ball down and he took the towel he wore on his hip, lifted the ball up, and you know how you wipe the baby, and then he picked it up and held it. It was cool. Then the big running back from the New York Giants, Brandon Jacobs, his wife was pregnant. So he scored and put the ball up under his jersey and doing like this in tribute to his wife or something. Brandon Marshall almost did the thing with the Obama gloves last season, where he had one white glove and one black one to represent the two sides meeting. That was cool.

Anyway, I'm still upset with ESPN that they didn't put the Hall of Fame jacket or the Riverdance or me doing CPR on the ball or jumping up with the cameraman or jumping into the Dawg Pound in Cleveland on those top 10 celebrations. All those deserved to be in the top 10. Like I said, they should do a top 10 of just my celebrations. I had a sweet dance after one against Pittsburgh one time. Real sweet.

Yeah, some old-school guys are like, "There's no place for that." Sorry, old-school, you don't like trash talk and having fun, here's the new school. Hell, I did a contest for Yahoo! Sports where we had fans send in their best touchdown dances. The stuff pretty much, well, it was kinda weak. But people loved doing it. They had a good time.

Even the coaches really understand. Like Marvin Lewis, my head coach, he doesn't care about most of that stuff. He thinks it's pretty fun. Now, he wasn't really into the Hall of Fame jacket thing, but that's cool. He told me what he thought. Hey, it happens.

When Hue Jackson was the receivers coach, I used to joke with him about the stuff I'd do. Sometimes I was joking with him. Sometimes I was checking out how much he would allow me to get away with. This is the way Hue looked at it: "You ask so much of guys in practice and during the week, during the off-season, to get prepared for a season, to focus on what we're trying to do, I have no problem with them celebrating a big play. The dances don't bother me as long as you're not making fun of the opponent. Now, there's times when Chad crosses the line and it's my job to keep him on the other side of that line. He'd sit there and say, 'I'm going to do this or that,' and I'd say, 'No, you're not.' Like one time he said he was going to score a touchdown and then grab the ref's flag from him and do something. No, you're not going to do that. Another time he said he was going to go kiss the ref. I said, 'No, you're not going to do that.' "

See, what I don't get is why the NFL makes a big deal out of it and in other cultures it's nothing. It's so much different here, because people get uptight about celebrations. You think the stuff I do in the NFL is out of control, it ain't nothing compared to how they are with soccer in Europe, their celebrations and their crazy hairstyles. I was hanging out with Thierry Henry, he said to me, "You'd just fit right in." But I couldn't do the soccer thing here. Fuck, no. Here, the money for soccer is horrible, and at a certain point, I was just too far along. You talk about being one of the best in the world, let's say I'm one of the best at receiver right now. I started when I was four years old. I stuck with football at some point when I realized that soccer wouldn't be the thing, and this is junior high going into high school. It wouldn't have done me no good to stick with soccer and then not have the means of being able to get all the way over to Europe anyway. My mind didn't think that way that young. Of course, my grandparents were like, "Please. Europe?

Yeah, right." Let alone I couldn't go around the damn corner. So you already know how that goes.

I still watch the game all the time. I have every soccer channel on DirecTV, I got the entire package. The celebrations when they score, awesome. If I played, I'd definitely be a striker. I gotta score, come on now. I gotta be able to celebrate. The ones they have over there are so sweet. They have so many because you've got all these different personalities. Everybody is different. So you always have different things. Some are very simple, but it's just like sweet. Some guys will do a cartwheel and then lift their shirt over their head. Just all kind of stuff. It's never over the top. Some people have seen my stuff and say it's over the top, but that's nothing. In Europe, they inspire me with some of the stuff that they do.

My favorite celebration is when Thierry Henry does his slide across the grass on his knees. The thing is that they water down the grass over there before the game, to keep the dust down and keep it cool. That makes the surface really smooth. So when he scores, he does this thing where he's running full speed and he drops on both knees and slides screaming at the same time. He's on his knees and he's got both fists balled up and he's screaming, and it is the sweetest thing. If I tried it, I'd burn my knees up and they'd fine my ass, big-time. But that is the best ever, that is so sweet. Totally just him going off with his emotions. It's the real deal.

It's so funny to get out and to be places and go places and meet different athletes from other sports, and people from different cultures, and then see the respect that they have for me. I'm in awe when I see them, and they're in awe when they see me. I'm like, "No, dude, do you know who you are and what you've done?" My stuff is nothing compared to them. It felt really good, especially to be in London and have certain people notice who you are. I'm all the way in London, and who would expect anyone to know who Chad Ochocinco was over there? To be able to sit out there in the box in the stadium and people come up and ask for autographs, that was an unbelievable feeling. It made me feel like all the stuff I do in games back home is cool with lots of people. We just don't understand that it's about having fun, entertaining people.

Hey, if you don't believe me, talk to the other players about it. Actually, I talked to them for you. Like safety Brian Dawkins, who has made the Pro Bowl seven times: "I like the dancing. Now, if everybody was doing that, it would be too much. But when you have different individuals doing different things, that shows that you have individuals doing things like that. That's the kind of stuff that brings in some fans. Not all fans are the same. Some fans hate that stuff. Other fans love it. So you have to bring in a little of all the fans. If he gets in the end zone, you never know what to expect from him. I appreciate him, his type of gamesmanship."

Or there's what Green Bay Pro Bowl cornerback Al Harris said: "No, no, no, it's fun and it makes the game fun. The outside world looks at what he does and doesn't understand it. But inside the game, he makes it fun. Guys are trying to compete and he's just getting everybody up."

But my favorite way of looking at it is what Ray Lewis had to say. He talked about how important it was as an expression of who we are as athletes. It's what makes us unique, he said: "That's what the game is, it's exciting. The number-one worst thing I hear is, 'Are you that football player?' No, I'm way more than being that football player. That's just what I do. That's what I do on Sunday, and when I do my thing and play well and want to celebrate, do it. Do it. You're not hurting nobody. Chad is not hurtin' nobody by celebrating. Is he? Is he showing somebody up by celebrating? No. It's the same thing as somebody sprinting down the field and throwing their arms in the air. It's the same exact celebration."

Hey, I know the fans love it. That's pretty damn obvious.

Now, lots of people want to know how I come up with the ideas. Hey, you got to be creative with this stuff, make it fun. It's like the year that I did the list of all the cornerbacks I was going up against that season, or how I sent the Cleveland secondary Pepto-Bismol that one year. You have to find ways to make it fun all the time.

Sometimes people come up to me with ideas. We had this one fan, a dancer dude, he named himself G, pretty typical. But he comes by doing this video of the SpongeBob Dance. Pretty funny. He was a little dude and his footwork was good. I was in sweats, so I really couldn't get it down the way I needed to, but you get ideas like that.

Oh, and I'll borrow somebody's dance, too. During that game I had 260 yards against San Diego, I did Shawne Merriman's "Lights Out" dance right in the middle of the game. That was a good one. As I was getting ready to do it, I yelled at Merriman, "Hey, Merriman, you'll like this one." He just laughed. Hey, you gotta keep it funny. You gotta keep talking to the guys.

Anyway, here's a look back at some of my best celebrations:

September 25, 2005, at Chicago: The Riverdance. Now, that was excellent. I worked on that the whole night before the game. T. J.

Houshmandzadeh, who was my roommate on the road at the time, kept watching me do it that night, helped me get it right.

Everybody thinks I did that because it came out the week that Bears linebacker Brian Urlacher's baby momma of his son, this woman named Tyria Robertson, had been sleeping with Michael Flatley, the Irish guy who came up with the Lord of the Dance. But that's not true. I would never do that. I was just coming up with a good idea. Seriously.

But that's some pretty crazy shit about this woman, and this is what I'm talking about with women when you're a player. You can't trust some women at all. They can really mess with your life if you're not careful. I feel bad for Urlacher. There are stories out there about him arguing with her and all that crap. What good is that for his kid, her throwing that stuff out there?

Now, some people might say I'm wrong, but you got to know about her. A year after this comes out, she ends up suing Flatley for like $33 million, claiming he raped her. Flatley proves that was a false accusation and then sues her for $11 million and wins. This stuff got out of control, man. Wow. Like I said, guys have to be careful.

Anyway, the Riverdance was cool. I was kind of disappointed I never heard from the Riverdance guys. I thought I was good. That day, after I scored my second touchdown, I did the push-up celebrations, a little dedication to my boy T. O.

The other thing is that later that season, when Pittsburgh came to play us, Steelers wide receiver Hines Ward copied the Riverdance. That was so fucking funny. I couldn't stop laughing. That was a good one.

November 20, 2005, at Indianapolis: The Proposal. They say when you propose it's supposed to take your breath away. Man, I was breathing heavy by the time I got to the sideline and saw the cheerleader. I had just scored on a 68-yard touchdown in a wild game against the Colts (we lost 45–37). We were up 14–10 and I race back to the sideline, run up to the cheerleader, this beautiful blond lady, drop down to one knee, and ask her right there. That was cool. She said yes.

Like I said, my inspiration on that one was from T. O., that time he went into the end zone and grabbed the pom-poms from the cheerleader and waved them. Pretty good, but I had to take it to the next level with the sign to T. O. Hue Jackson thinks I got a date out of that one. I'll let y'all guess on that one. Hey, you don't need to know all my business.

Now, here's where I think I deserve some credit. Do they give a brother like me some love when I do something good? Of course not.

A little over a year later, what happens in the Tostitos Fiesta Bowl? The dude Ian Johnson from Boise State runs for the two-point conversion on the trick play (pretty sweet play), runs out of bounds, goes up to his girlfriend the cheerleader, and proposes. She's so happy she jumps into his arms, he's all over ESPN, even made the national news, but does he send a shout-out to his boy Ochocinco for giving him the idea? No. Do I get an invite to the wedding? No. I even would have bought him a nice set of china and everything.

Now, there's another idea, Ochocinco china. You could have a beautiful set of dishes with an impression of me either on the plate itself or all around the edge.

December 14, 2003, at Cincinnati: Please Don't Fine Me Again. Of course, what did NFL Commissioner Paul Tagliabue do? He fined me $10,000 for that one. This was about the time that me and T. O. and Joe Horn were taking celebrations to a whole new level. In 2002, T. O. pulled the Sharpie celebration, which is a classic.

Then, early in 2003, I got fined $5,000 twice. The first time was when me and Peter Warrick, an old teammate of mine in Cincinnati, struck a photo pose in the end zone after a touchdown in Cleveland on September 28. Then I got another $5,000 fine for making a throat-slash gesture following a score against Seattle on October 26. The NFL got all serious about the throat slash, but guys had been doing that one for years and that's an old wrestling move. I mean, come on.

So I go through the rest of the season and I'm trying to think about something, but I can't really come up with anything great. A couple of spontaneous things, like when I scored three touchdowns in San Diego and did the Shawne Merriman dance.

We get home against the 49ers and I come up with my idea. I bury this sign in the end zone that says: "Dear NFL, Please Don't Fine Me Again." Nice sign with black letters on orange paper, Bengals colors. That's pretty funny. I'm not going to dance or anything, but I bury it in the snow in one end zone and I was ready to go for it when I scored. It's right in the first quarter, I catch a 10-yard touchdown pass and go get my sign. I mean, come on, I didn't really do anything like a pose or a dance. That's funny.

The league thought they were going to get me to back down, but you can't stop Ocho. It's like I said that week when the league announced the fine: "It's OK. I've got two more games left [this season]—that's two more fines, then I'm finished for the rest of my career with the fines."

Yeah, right.

But the best part of that one was later that night, the New York Giants are playing New Orleans and Joe Horn goes off. Nine catches, 133 yards, and four touchdowns, and the Saints crush them 45–7. After his second touchdown, Horn gets the cell phone out from the padding on the goalpost and makes a call. That's a classic and then they fine Joe $30,000 for it. Man, that's wrong. I liked that one. We were taking it to a whole new level.

October 9, 2005, at Jacksonville: CPR on the Ball. Now, some people didn't really get this one, but this was a couple of weeks after Chicago, so I was kind of rolling. I scored against the Jaguars, put the ball down, and pretended to give it CPR. Hey, I'm trying to save a life here!

November 27, 2005, at Cincinnati: The Tiger Woods Fist Pump. Now, this is clever, right? We're in the middle of this huge win against Baltimore, 42–29, on the way to the playoffs and I catch a 54-yard touchdown pass, put the ball on the ground, grab the pylon, and putt the ball. I give it the Tiger Woods fist pump. What's the problem with that? We're up 17–0 and we were rolling to a 34–0 lead. I didn't even get flagged for that, but the league fined me $5,000.

That game was against Dale Carter, who I know from South Florida, and Deion Sanders was playing for Baltimore, too. I had to give those guys a little something special.

Later that season, I had a couple of nice ones. At Detroit, I did what people called "Understated Chad," kind of mocked myself. Then we played at home on Christmas Eve against Buffalo. After I scored in that game, I grabbed a big Santa stocking and threw candy canes to the fans. Hey, I'm big on the holidays.

But think about that season. I had Riverdance, the push-ups, CPR, and the Tiger Woods all going in one season. We also went to the playoffs that season, so I guess all my celebrations didn't really hurt us, did they?

Anyway, that's got to be like Hall of Fame stuff, right? I deserve to go to Canton on that alone. Speaking of the Hall of Fame . . .

September 10, 2007, at Cincinnati: Hall of Fame Class of 20?? This has to be my favorite one. I got that idea from watching the Hall of Fame induction thing with Michael Irvin the month before. I just thought, since I'm going to be there at some point, why not? I think a lot of people liked it, some people thought it was corny, but my whole thing is I think it's funny. Every time I say something or every time I do something, there's a funny message to it, whether you think so or not. One day I'm going to be in the Hall of Fame, whether you like it or not. When I get inducted, I'm going to pull out that old jacket that everybody laughed about and made fun of, the one that said "20??" I'm going to keep it until then, and then I'll be like, "I told you so."

When I get inducted, I'm going to have that wonderful speech, and then I'll have to practice on my crying so I'll have tears coming down like Michael Irvin. I was feeling that. It was a good speech. Will I do a celebration dance? At that time, I might not be able to walk, I might be on crutches. Who knows, I've got to have something special, so you never know. I just can't be inducted without any type of flash. It will probably be something nice. Whatever it is, it will probably be the best speech of all time. Then they will probably change the rule for all Hall of Famers who get up to talk—you will not be allowed to do this anymore.

I know, I know, I took a lot of shit from the old-school guys for this, and my coaches, Marvin Lewis, Bob Bratkowski, and Hue Jackson, weren't real happy. They were telling me about how sacred and special that is, how the guys there take it so seriously, it's like the Holy Grail. Look, Holy Grail or not, I'm going to be there.

But dude, the other thing was, this was Monday Night Football, season-opening game. Do you know how big this game is? I had to have something special. This was unreal. I'm trying to get us geeked up for this game and I start us off with the touchdown, sweet 39-yarder, beat the fuck out of Chris McAlister again, and we're on our way to a 27–20 victory, which is freakin' huge for us. Too bad the rest of the season kind of sucked, but that's another story.

But I'm telling you, I'm going to be there. I'm going to be in the Hall of Fame. I'm the best out there, and by the time I'm done, it's going to be sick. I'm serious, totally sick, the numbers I put up, what I do. The only thing is I got to win. I got to be on a team that wins to make it all worth it. But the Hall of Fame? As I put it on the jacket, it's not a matter of if, it's only about when.

September 16, 2007, at Cleveland: The Dawg Pound Leap. OK, this might actually be one I sort of regret. Not so much because we lost in one of my biggest games (11 catches, 209 yards, and we drop this one 51–45). That sucked enough, but when I jumped into the Dawg Pound after I scored a touchdown, I knew the guys there would catch me, even though they like to scream every name in the book at me. See, you can tell those dudes are having fun.

Those guys are what the NFL is about, guys sitting in the end zone, dressing up in dog faces, painting their chests, screaming and hollering. Those guys have had a brutal week at work and want to be entertained.

They love me, even if I play for the Bengals. They need me, man. I'm like therapy for them.

I just didn't think one dude would pour beer on me. You can see it right after I make the leap. The dude to my left leans right over, pours his beer right on me. Considering that beer probably cost him $8, I gotta think that's some pretty strong feelings of hate.

Anyway, even though most of the dudes in the Dawg Pound were cool about me leaping up there, I smelled like beer the rest of the game. That sucked. It was hot, so by the end of the game, I smelled like a frat house at 5 A.M. Not good.

November 25, 2007, at Cincinnati: The Cameraman. This was a good one, but it took forever for me to do. I was on a roll with ideas, but I wasn't on a roll at getting into the end zone. I went eight games without a touchdown. Eight games? I shouldn't go eight minutes without a touchdown. Aside from my rookie year and 2008, that was the longest I'd ever gone without getting into the end zone. So I'm just waiting and waiting and waiting to pull this great idea.

Finally, I have the big game against Tennessee. I score three touchdowns and we blow out Tennessee 35–6. Sweet game and I had to show it. I score on a 10-yard touchdown in the first half, run right through the end zone, jump up on the camera nest, and take over the controls.

And I got a 15-yard penalty for that? The camera isn't a prop. It's part of the game.

Hey, where would the NFL be without the cameras?

Chad's not a hard guy to coach. Yeah, you have to be on top of your game with him. He's pushing you just like you're pushing him. Sometimes you just have to be ready to put your foot up his ass once in a while to get his attention.

—**Hue Jackson,** former Cincinnati Bengals
wide receivers coach

NINE

BELICHICK AND THE OTHER COACHES

BILL BELICHICK IS SO funny. I was in the Pro Bowl after the 2006 season and he was the coach. He told me that when we played the next season, the Bengals and Patriots, "You are not going to catch anything, because we are going to triple your ass when you play." So we play the Patriots that next season and I catch like two or three passes early in the game. He looked at me and I talked to him at the sidelines. He told me, "I can't believe this shit. I told you, you wouldn't catch anything and you started running through my guys." He was so pissed off.

I loved it and he was smiling, laughing a little. I could tell he was a little serious and a little not. Belichick likes to talk a little trash, but it's all in fun. There are a lot of coaches I have love for. Belichick is the best. You can see that. I don't care about all that stuff they say about him cheating. He knows the game and the players can see it. When you're a player, that's what you ask for, a coach who is going to put you in the right situation and knows what to do.

I hear people talk about Spygate this and Spygate that. You hear guys from Pittsburgh complain about how the Patriots knew what the fuck they were doing and how they would have beaten them. Spygate, my ass. Take those cameras away and you are going to get the same goddamn results. The Patriots are good. They don't have the most talent, we all know that. They don't have the most speed, no question. But there's a reason why they are winning even though everybody is over age 50. It's the fucking coaching. It ain't no secret. It's obvious. People use the Spygate thing as an excuse. What are they going to say this year? No cameras now, no Spygate now. But when the Patriots continue to win week in and week out, what's everybody going to say now? You tell me what it is. They're lucky I didn't come out and say that back in 2007 after all that shit came out. The media would have killed me. He might be the greatest coach that ever coached.

Did they have cameras after the first week of the 2007 season? No, and what did they do? They almost went undefeated. If David Tyree doesn't make the greatest, most ridiculously awesome catch in the history of the game, New England goes 19–0. Shit, just the fact that they went 18–1 should have been enough for everybody to just back the fuck off of Belichick. And it wasn't like they were just squeaking by people. They were *killing* it. It was ugly.

They were beating teams by like 17, 20, 21, 46 points. They put up 48, 49, and 56 points . . . on the road. I mean, that's humiliating teams in their own place. And you could tell, they meant it. It was take-no-prisoners shit. They were burning the huts and stealing the women. It was mean and it was intense.

They came to our place on a Monday night. I catch a few balls, get on Belichick's case, he gives me some shit, but it's not like he was taking me all that serious. He was like just messing around. "Oh yeah, Chad, you're doing great, blah, blah, blah." Meanwhile, they kind of get control of the game. They're up 24–10 going into the fourth quarter. Randy Moss already has a touchdown catch, Brady already has some big numbers.

They're still up 27–13 after we trade field goals. They're at their own 15-yard line, bad field position. There's like nine minutes left in the game. Most teams would kind of sit on it right there, maybe try to get a field goal, but make sure they run the clock, don't take too many chances with the ball.

Not them. Not Belichick, not Brady, not Moss. Pass, pass, pass, pass, pass. They're working the clock a little, staying in bounds, but the first pass is a long throw to Moss for 20 yards and then they just keep coming. By the time they're done throwing, they're at our 26-yard line and now it's like they stuck the knife in our back and they're just turning it. They were stupid good.

BILL BELICHICK
New England Patriots head coach

I first met Chad when he was coming out of college. We were at USC for a workout with him because he was living in Los Angeles. So he drives into the USC campus with all this Oregon State stuff on his car. It's like those metallic flags that they stick to the side of the car, shit like that. I look at him and say, "Chad, what are you thinking? Somebody is going to take a key and put like a four-scratch in your car. Put that stuff away." He says, "You're probably right." Anyway, he ran routes that day and he ran all day. He would run routes for four hours if you asked him. You could just see it, he loves football. They had some former USC backup quarterback out there trying to get a look, and Chad would have run as long as that guy wanted to throw.

Then, when we met at the Pro Bowl [in 2006], it was great. Him and [current New England linebacker] Adalius Thomas would gather the AFC players together after practice and they'd tell some real off-color joke to get everybody cracked up. I don't think you want to include these jokes in the book, let me say that. But it would be one of those every day just to get everybody laughing. They were fun. In practice, it was even better. He has fun and he really competes. All the time. You know how Pro Bowl practices are. It wouldn't have been half-speed without Chad pushing it. We had Rashean Mathis and Champ Bailey out there at corner in practice, and Chad would run a route, catch a pass, spike it at their feet, and start talking to them. He wanted them to be up for practice. It would go that way a couple more plays and then Chad would say: "I'm going to run a fucking in cut and I'm still going to catch it on you. I'm going to tell you what I'm going to do and I'm still going to do it." With him it's never half-speed.

It was a one-on-one thing where he had to get the other guy going to feel like he was into it. He has a lot of fun competing, and you can see that. Anyway, that week goes on and we're having a good time. Then we get to game day and the NFC gets in its bus and the AFC gets in its bus going to the stadium. It's like a 40- or 45-minute drive from the hotel to the stadium. It's almost like being in a high school game. Anyway, after about five minutes, the NFC bus breaks down and we're all stopped. There's smoke coming out of the bus. The NFL is trying to get people out there, but after about 10 minutes the NFC guys just pile into our bus. Everybody is cramped in or standing up. Chad ends up sitting next to me and we're talking the whole time. That kid loves life, let me tell you. You can see it, and it really comes out on the field.

Anyway, I tell him that we're going to double the shit out of him when we played that year and, of course, we did double him. I think Carson Palmer threw one out of bounds on our sideline. He comes over and yells, "Goddamn it." So I say to him, "You can't catch a ball on us, the only way you can get open is to push off, that's all you ever do, push off." Just giving him a little crap, having a good time with him. Really, I don't have that relationship with a lot of guys in the NFL who are not on our team. Chad is unique, he's fun. He's a really good guy who enjoys himself. Yeah, he's loud, but he likes to be coached. He cares. He comes back, listens to what you have to say, and really tries to do the things you're talking to him about. It's like with the celebrations, with some of those guys, it's all about themselves and you can see it. You can tell the difference. He's just trying to have some fun with it after he's done something meaningful and I respect that.

Well, Bill and I have a little difference of opinion on what was said, but that's cool. I'll let him believe that. Back to the game: Now that they're in field-goal range to really put it away, they run three times and even force us to use a time-out with 3:24 left. What happens? It's third-and-5 at our 14-yard line, you figure they run one more time, force us to use a time-out, and then kick the field goal to put us out of our misery.

Nope, they line up in shotgun formation and Brady throws to Moss for a 14-yard touchdown. They wanted to kill people. I'm like, "Man, why did everybody have to go piss them off with that Spygate crap? What, like they weren't good enough already?" They beat us 34–13.

Now, some people around the league were saying stuff like, "They're just trying to embarrass us, that's not right." I'm like, shut the fuck up. This is the NFL, man. This ain't Pop Warner or high school. Either you stop them or you score and keep up. I don't blame them one bit for running it up, especially when everybody is trying to say stupid shit like their titles are tainted. Tainted? Let me tell you, I know how hard it is just to get to the playoffs. I don't care if you know the signals, winning three Super Bowls and getting to a fourth one is serious.

Plus, what is everybody complaining about with New England stealing the signals? It's not like people didn't know. Change the signals. Do something different. It's not that hard to change one word in a call.

What the Patriots are better at than everybody is knowing what to do. Like I said, they have all these 50-something-year-old guys on defense who are smart as hell. Tedy Bruschi, Mike Vrabel, Junior Seau, Richard Seymour. I don't know what they do, but I can tell you that they're in the right spot all the time. They have to be, because their secondary ain't anything great. Rodney Harrison is good, even if he's always trying to intimidate you. That stuff doesn't work with me, because I'm never letting him get a good shot at me. I'm too smart for that.

With New England, they're never going to beat themselves. You're going to have to make a play against them, and their offense is always going to put pressure on you now that Brady has Moss and all those dudes.

Even last season, they lose Brady in the first game of the season and they go 11–5. Oh yeah, and they lost Adalius Thomas and Bruschi and Harrison, all these dudes. Think about that. I've been in Cincinnati for eight years and our *best* season is 11–5. The Pats lose the MVP of the league from 2007 after seven and a half minutes of the season and they go 11–5. They do it with a quarterback who hasn't started a game since high school. High school?

Yeah, Matt Cassel. He was Carson Palmer's backup at USC, then had to back up Matt Leinart for two years. The dude can't get a sniff. Gets drafted by the Patriots, sits around watching Brady for three years, and then plays like he's been out there the whole time.

That's why I say, if you asked any player in this league, he'd tell you, "I want to play for Bill Belichick." Anybody. Any guy who says otherwise is lying his ass off. Yeah, some guys are pissed about Spygate. You know what I say? Get over it. They'd still want Belichick and they know it.

Belichick does exactly what a player wants a coach to do. He puts you in the right situation to have success. As a player, that's all you ask. Put me in the right situation and then it's all on me as the player. If I don't get it done, my bad. And here's the other thing about Belichick, he's not just working one side of the ball.

Everybody used to say that he was just some defensive guru, a defensive genius, and that he let somebody else do the offense. That's so wrong. He knows both sides of the ball. More important, he knows how to fix mistakes in a hurry.

Now, you can tell me they haven't won a title since Charlie Weis or whoever the fuck that dude was who ran the offense, but let's look at it the other way. What has Weis done since he left New England? The dude goes to Notre Dame and now they hate his ass, they think he doesn't know shit. He loses Brady Quinn, who everybody thought was Tom Brady Jr., and now Notre Dame sucks.

Meanwhile, Belichick totally changes his offense in two years. After 2005, he lets David Givens and Deion Branch go because he thinks that receivers are interchangeable. He finds out in 2006 that you better have some dudes who can play and trades for Moss, Wes Welker, and Donte Stallworth. Throw in Jabar Gaffney and you got a damn nice receiving corps. I mean, that's pretty serious. Almost as good as me, T. J., and Chris Henry.

And Belichick comes out slaughtering people. Shit, Josh McDaniels, that dude who looks like he's 14 who was offensive coordinator, don't tell me he was running the offense for Belichick. No way. Belichick knew everything that was going on. He was in the quarterback meetings, he talks directly to Brady, and those guys are on the same page. You can see that. You read the stories. He's going to see the Florida coach, Urban Meyer, learning about the spread offense. He's putting the spread offense into his playbook. Belichick is like a football-thinking machine.

Or like this. Belichick realizes what happened in 2006, rebuilds the offense in 2007, and then lets those dudes fly. Brady throws 50 touchdown passes. Moss catches 23 TD passes. They're setting records every week. I mean, that's all Belichick making aggressive, big-time moves.

Then he loses Brady the next year and still almost makes the playoffs. Ridiculous. Best coach in the league.

But there's lots of coaches I get along with. Belichick, Herm Edwards, Tony Dungy. I love these dudes. There's something special about them outside of this. I don't know what it is. I love watching Herm running on the sideline before games, looking like he's still ready to ball. He gives you that look, kinda like, "Are you crazy?" and then he breaks out in a big smile. Tony would be so cool to play for. Nothing bothers him. He's totally under control.

Now, everybody who thinks that's a dig at Marvin Lewis, don't be stupid. Marvin is a damn good coach, but Marvin doesn't have control of the football team the same way Belichick has control. No way. Belichick runs everything in New England when it comes to the football team and the owner stays out of the way. That's not the case in Cincinnati. I know there are things that Marvin would want to do if he was in charge. We'd have a way different setup, that's all I know.

I have a lot of love for Marvin, despite what everybody thinks on the outside. All that stuff he said in the 2007 off-season about how he wished me well if I retired, people don't understand. He has to say stuff like that. He knows what's going on with me. He knows what I'm thinking. There's no animosity or anything like that. Man, I call him at three o'clock in the morning sometimes. We have a different relationship than everybody thinks. The outside doesn't know stuff like that.

They want to say me and my coach don't get along. That's why the coaches feel so bad about what's going on right now and what everybody is saying about how we supposedly don't get along. It's like the retirement thing. When Marvin said that, it went in one ear and out the other for me. Yeah, some guys might take offense to that. Me, I don't care. I didn't pay that any mind. I knew what he had to do, to take his stand for the team and his organization. He has to do that or management is going to be upset.

And people don't understand, you can get into it with your coach and that doesn't mean you don't still respect him. This season, Marvin and I got into it big-time one day. He didn't think I was hustling, running full-go on one play, and all of a sudden he says, "What the fuck is going on with you?" I'm like, "What the fuck is going on with me? What the fuck is going on with you?" All of a sudden it's "Well, fuck you." "No, fuck you." We're just going at it. That was a good one.

And, like I said, the only thing a player can ask is that a coach puts him in the best position to succeed, and that's what all of those guys have done in my career. Except for this year—and I know I made my bed—those guys have made sure I got the ball. I got my chances to do my thing.

Like I said, that's why I love those guys.

Same thing with my old wide receivers coach, Hue Jackson. I love Hue, he's one of my three or four favorite coaches. That's why people who think I got into a fight with him or Marvin or whoever in that playoff game against Pittsburgh, they have no clue. Do you really think I would have been playing in the second half if I had taken a swing at one of them? Hell no. I was upset and I was going to go talk to our offensive coordinator [Bob Bratkowski]. But I'm sitting on the table with an IV in my arm and I get up to go and pull the IV out of my arm, there's blood, and all of a sudden Hue is holding me back, calming me down.

But Hue and me, we fight and cuss and we get along. He was always just pushing me to get the best out of me. That's it. It's like in practice one day, I'm not warmed up yet and he thinks I should be running full-go on a deep route. I'm like, "I'm not ready." He says, "Well, if you can't run full-go, get the fuck off the field." I'm like, "I'll go full-go when I'm warmed up, I'm not goin' anywhere." He says, "Get the fuck off the field." I say, "Fuck no, I'm not going." That was another good one. We were really going at it good. But that's how we get on each other. They're pushing me to be my best. I want to be my best.

Hue Jackson, he was my receiving coach with the Bengals, and now he's in Baltimore. Yeah, everybody talks about how we supposedly got into it during the playoff game. Yeah, we had a problem, but that's the biggest game of our lives right there. We finally made the playoffs and we lost our quarterback early in that game. I'm pissed and I don't want to be the sitting duck, fuck that. Let's find a way, because I'm going to find a way. That's why they are playing me the way they are, because they know what's going to happen if they don't. They have to take me away. I'm in the locker room at halftime and I'm saying I want y'all to have that same attitude. The Pittsburgh defense is saying, "We're taking Chad out of the game." I'm saying to my teammates, "I want y'all to be like, you know what, y'all aren't stopping our 85." That's how I want you to play the game—like that, with that attitude.

And my coaches can be totally honest with me, not just in private, but in public. They say exactly what they think. It's like what Coach Bratkowski said after the playoff game. He told me right then I was a distraction. He told me, "Hey, we're winning this game. When you come in here screaming and hollering, everybody lost focus." Hey, I thought about that, but I was intense about it and I let him know what I was thinking. A couple of days later, when the news came out that I lost my cool and that I supposedly took a swing at Marvin or Hue or whatever they were saying in the media, I said that shit wasn't true, none of that happened. Brat called me up right away and he told me that was bull- shit, that he thought I lied. I listened to him, I heard him out. I still love him. I know he wants me to be the best.

Hey, I know that it was Brat who stood up for me with the Bengals when I didn't get drafted in the first round. I know what happened. He stood up on that table and told the team that they needed to take a chance on me when everybody else in the NFL was saying, "Oh, the guy has never been one place for more than a year, you can't trust him, his one year was a flash in the pan." Hey, I know what I did to my chances, and Brat helped bail me out. He stood up for me. If he can do that, I better listen to what he has to say, whether I like it or not.

If players want to change their name to Michelin Tires, then that's what you need to put on the back of the jersey, Michelin Tires. Right or wrong, that's a player's right. He can change his name. Yeah, it's absurd, but at the same time, if he did it the right way, it could be good. It's funny, because it's Ochocinco who thought of doing it, but if he can make money doing it, let him. Hey, they gonna stop paying us one day, and while you can get it, get all you can. When it's over, it's over. He ain't going to be this popular when he's done playing.

—**Joey Porter,** Miami Dolphins Pro Bowl linebacker

TEN

OCHOCINCO, MARKETING GENIUS

YES, I AM A marketing genius. If you don't believe me, let's ask an expert.

In October 2007, Yahoo! public relations manager Nicol Addison stood in front of more than 130 members of the Yahoo.com staff at the sports department retreat in Las Vegas and made all of them laugh.

It was easy—she had me to help her. Not literally, I wasn't there in Vegas. Man, can you imagine me in Vegas? I'd take over the town, I'd be bigger than Penn & Teller and Celine Dion and Siegfried & Roy combined. Forget Ocean's 11, 12, and 13, Chad Ochocinco is on the way. I'm like Sinatra and Sammy all rolled into one.

Damn, I digress a lot. Anyway, my girl Nicol from Yahoo! is amped for this presentation she's going to do in front of her colleagues. Why? 'Cause she has Ochocinco on her side, that's why. That year, I was the spokesman for Yahoo! Sports fantasy football. Hell, I am fantasy football. I got the stats, I got the big plays. If you're picking a team for fantasy football, I'm your guy. Anyway, I aced the ad that Nicol had me do that year. Better yet, we did a whole separate contest for Yahoo! for fans to come up with their best celebration, make a video, and send it to Yahoo!. This was sweet. They called it the Chad Johnson Touchdown Celebration Showdown. It ran for like 12 days and got hundreds of entries. The nickname for it was Project Ocho Cinco.

But more on that later. Back to Vegas. You see, Nicol was geeked up about this because the previous time she'd worked with an athlete, it was Johnny Damon of the Yankees. I don't know if Nicol wants me to get into this, but that didn't go so well from what I hear. I actually watched the spot. Damon said some shit like, "Yahoo! Fantasy Baseball . . . why not?" I'm like, what the fuck is that? Are you serious? They pay you money to be a spokesman and that's all you could come up with? What do you expect, he's a baseball player.

Anyway, you want to know how good I was? Well, ask Nicol:

NICOL ADDISON
Yahoo! public relations manager

Chad Johnson, love him! He was one of the best athletes I've worked with. My first meeting with him was when [our] crew filmed the promotional video. He arrived by himself and on time, not something I was used to when working with athletes. He was so pleasant, I immediately got that he understood the business side of his profession by the way he handled the session. I was shocked by this because my Chad Johnson perception had been tainted by what I saw on

YouTube—the "Ochocinco" videos, the gold teeth, and the Mohawk. I really wasn't sure what I was getting, but after the first two minutes I was a Chad Johnson fan. A fan of Chad Johnson the athlete; Chad Johnson the brand; Chad Johnson the businessman; and Chad Johnson the fan favorite. The rest of the promotion included Chad signing autographs for the Yahoo! team, media training, radio interviews, and a visit with the winner [of the Yahoo! celebration contest, Anthony Nappi]. Chad aced them all. The highlight was the fan visit, Anthony was so excited to meet Chad, and Ochocinco did not let him down. Chad wowed the winner with his charm, including doing the actual winning celebration with the guy, several times; turning it on for the cameras, and after the cameras left, Chad took the winner on a tour of the locker room. He concluded Anthony's visit of a lifetime by giving him an autographed pair of shoes and a game ball. This is why fans love him—behind the talk and the bravado, he is a great guy that delivers on his brand in a way fans can relate to. I love him!

If you don't think that's enough, listen to what Nappi, the dude who won the competition, said. Good dude. I had this great moment with him when he came to Cincinnati. It was on a Friday and I was tired. We were playing terrible, so I couldn't be celebrating all that much. How do you celebrate when you're playing bad? We were horrible. Anyway, I meet Anthony and we're goofing around for the cameras and stuff and I can tell he has something he really wants to say. So finally, he gets comfortable enough with what we're doing that he says what he's been thinking about. Now, he's a teacher and kind of a short white guy, but he's cool and I can see he's having a great time. So I listen.

Nappi: "When you celebrate 'cause you're excited and you just scored a touchdown, everyone feeds off that. Not just your fans, but the team, the city. To not celebrate a touchdown is like you saying, 'I'm not going to be Chad Ochocinco, I'm going to be somebody else.' "

Now he's getting me to thinking. I'm a little too tired to be all fired up, but I get it and he kind of got me excited. It was cool. I hesitate just a little, look at the camera, and say, "I'm back celebrating." After that, I was doing a TV interview by myself and told them: "To hear what he told me about not really being a fan [of the Bengals], but watching the game because of me—and I've heard that a lot and needed to hear it again—it's very special to hear that, especially at a time like this."

Anyway, for all those people who think I'm such an asshole, here's what this dude thought after the meeting.

ANTHONY NAPPI
professor, St. Petersburg College, Florida

That weekend was great. It was a lot more than I had anticipated and more than he was contracted to do. The only thing he had to do was spend an hour with me. That's all he was obligated to do. He was supposed to come out on the field [at Paul Brown Stadium], hang out on the field with me, have me show him the winning entry from the contest, and have him practice it a couple of times. Really, I wasn't sure what to expect, because once I arrived there, he was under a lot of turmoil at the time about whether he should be celebrating. He was catching a lot of flak from the city, ESPN, Mike Ditka, a lot of people were coming down on him.

I could definitely see how it hurt him. He was visibly upset. He was really stressed when he was talking at first. But as we got to talking and we were standing there in front of the reporters who were doing a story about it, he got into it and he really seemed to be having fun and he made it great for me. Then I gave him that speech I'd been thinking—basically, you rode in on that horse and you need to keep riding that horse. I told him he shouldn't stop being who he was just because the team might not be doing well.

To me, he transcends the hard-core football fan and appeals to the more casual fan who may not understand the game on a complex level. He's able to connect to those people because of his larger-than-life personality. He transcends the game. I don't like to put him in the same light as a guy like Terrell Owens, who doesn't seem to be a good guy, but he's more than just the regular star. I'm not the first person to say that, but I wanted to reinforce in him this is why I like to watch him play. Well, anyway, I was there for a while and I showed him a couple of other celebrations I had come up with that I had actually entered. It was odd, because the celebration I did, which was called the "Shot Put" because I was spinning like a shot-putter and tossing the ball, I didn't think was my best idea. I had a couple of other ideas for celebrations, but I waited for about 45 minutes, when the cameras finally left, before I showed him. I don't know if he actually remembered it or not later that season, but I had the idea for him to commandeer the camera after he scored, give the football to the cameraman, have the cameraman spike it, and film the defensive coordinator from the other team as the coordinator reacted to the touchdown. I brought that one up and I was shocked later that season when he actually did it. It really felt good to think, "Hey, maybe he remembered my idea." I'd love to think I could come up with creative ideas like that and maybe make a living doing stuff like that, but that's not realistic. I used to come up with nicknames for guys for Chris Berman with ESPN. He's probably used 10 or 12 of them over the years. With Chad, I had a little playbook of celebrations and showed him a couple of other ideas. I had another one for a fine bucket, where he scores, celebrates, and then gets this giant bucket out to pass around to the fans to help pay for the fine. Not really collect money, just pretend.

So we were there for the hour, and Nicol stepped in and said, "OK, anything else?" I thought we were all done, but then he just looked at me and said, "You know what, come with me." That's when he took me to the locker room and showed me around. I was shocked because he looked exhausted and he had been saying that all he wanted to do was go home and go to sleep. But he took me to the locker room, showed me the training room, introduced me to a few players who were still hanging around. He showed me his locker. Then he pulls out a pair of shoes and signs them and just gives them to me. I was like, "You don't have to do that." He's already signed a bunch of other stuff, like the little helmets and a bunch of things I had to bring home. But he said to me, "Nah, don't worry about it. I appreciate you didn't just come here and ask me for things. That's what happens most of the time." I could see that he gets that a lot, people pulling at him, always wanting something. I asked him about it and he said, "Yeah, it's hard, but it's what comes with the territory." He didn't like it, but he didn't want to give it up and not play football.

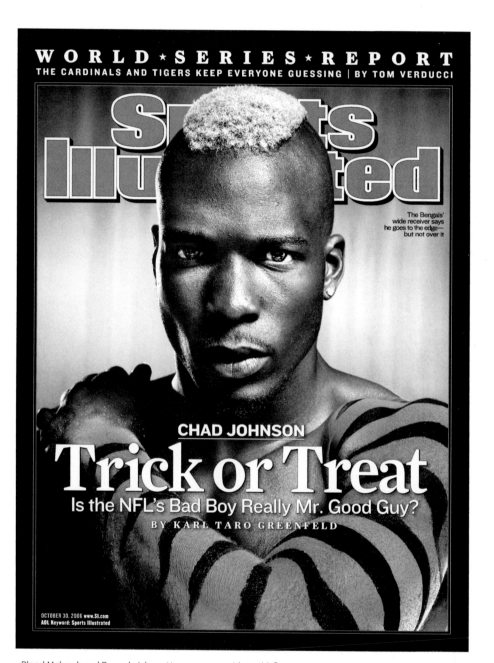

Blond Mohawk and Bengal stripes. How can you not love this? *Michael J. LeBrecht II/Sports Illustrated/Getty Images*

Ray Lewis is the guy so many players look to for guidance. He has been through it all. He helped me get through everything after the 2007 season, and I still call him all the time. *Ned Dishman/Getty Images*

Nice form on this putt, and you should have seen the fist pump after I made the shot. I had my salute to Tiger Woods down pat. Now, I just need a few lessons from Tiger to get my game straight. *AP Photo/ Tony Tribble*

This was after my TD catch in Cleveland. Now, I know everybody loves me, but the dude could have just handed me the beer. *Gregory Shamus/Getty Images*

I caught this touchdown over Rashean Mathis of Jacksonville. As I said before, Rashean who? *AP Photo/ Tony Tribble*

Nice touchdown catch for me over Bryant McFadden of Pittsburgh. But the Steelers got what I really want, championships. *AP Photo/Tony Tribble*

This catch was against the Ravens, I think. I do this so much I kinda forget. You throw it, I'll get it.
Dan Beineke/NFL/Getty Images

This is the kind of stuff that fans just don't understand. In football, everybody is emotional, so you end up yelling and screaming at each other every game. But it doesn't mean anything. It's just part of Sunday. *AP Photo/Tony Tribble*

That's me with Who Dey, the Bengals mascot. He should actually be my own personal mascot. All I ever say about opponents is, "Who dey?" *AP Photo/Tony Tribble*

This is me and my boy C.J. He's running track and playing football now, just like I did.

I was best man at the wedding of my good friend Rashad Thomas. By my side is one of my best girls, my daughter Gigi.

Me and my daughters. That's Chadé on my shoulders, and then Gigi is standing with Chaiel on her shoulders. Good-looking, happy girls. I might have trouble on my hands. I probably deserve it.

Yeah, this is what I'm talking about. Football, Ping-Pong, it doesn't matter. I will rule the world in all sports.

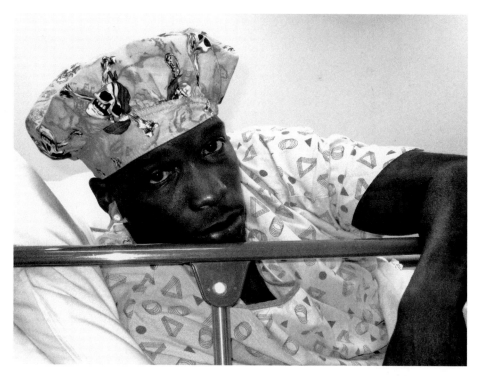

So here's the story on the pirate surgical cap, which I wore when I had my ankle scoped before 2008. They wanted me to go into surgery with the plain surgical cap on. I'm like, "Hell no, I gotta have some style." So they found this one in the children's wing. Cool.

This is me on TRL in 2008. I should do more TV for real. Put me on *The Real World*, I'd be the greatest character they ever had. I'd turn that show upside down. House party every night. Imagine the ratings.

Scott Gries/Getty Images

These are my Malcolm X glasses. A little old-school, but very cool and edgy.

I love the glasses. I collect 'em, got a thousand pairs, help me with any mood at any time. Got to have a little fun.

When you live a life like mine, you gotta get a little sleep whenever and wherever you can.

Then, when we went into the training room, the equipment guys were working on the footballs for the game, scuffing them up according to [quarterback] Carson Palmer's specifications, getting them ready for the game. Chad grabbed a brand-new game ball, signed it, and handed it to me. I've got a pair of shoes, a new football. Then he walked me out to the car and you could hear people trying to hound him for stuff. He ended up spending like an hour and 45 minutes, almost two hours with me and my girlfriend, who's now my fiancée. He was just amazingly gracious and really seemed to want to be good about making sure I enjoyed myself. I really appreciated it.

Again, he didn't have to do any of it. But he was very genuine, very caring. It wasn't like he was even trying to impress the people from Yahoo! He just did it, took me to some off-limits places. He went above and beyond what he needed to do with a complete stranger. It's not like I was someone from the Make-A-Wish Foundation or someone with a debilitating illness. But I was really impressed, because it changed any image I might have had of him. You read negative things about a person, bad press about people, but then meet them and realize you don't really understand the exact situation. Meeting him changed the way I look at people. I'm not saying he's perfect, but he was so gracious and giving of his time.

I still have a digital photo album of that weekend and I look at it all the time. I'm just a Chad Ochocinco fan, not a Bengals fan. The Green Bay Packers are my team, and on Sundays I'll go over to my dad's house with my brother and the three of us will watch the Packers. But every chance I get, I switch to the Bengals to see if there are any highlights of Chad, something he has done. Really, the first time

I noticed him was the Riverdance. I said, "Hey, look at this guy, he's
different." I thought it was hysterical, it was just neat to see a player
with creativity to go with his talent. He definitely has a life after football, with his talent and his personality.

See what I'm saying? Now, this is what I don't understand: If I get it, why
does the league not understand that I can only help them? I should be
like an ambassador for the NFL. They should send me to Europe and
China and Mexico to promote the game.

But what does the NFL really do to me? Well, they fine me all the
time for trying to entertain the people with the celebrations. They make
rules about the celebrations all the time. They do everything to take the
fun out of it. Like the players say, it's the No Fun League. But you want
to know the truth? They love it, they love the bad boys, the guys who
push the limits. Everybody knows that. When I saw NFL Commissioner
Roger Goodell before last season, I told him I had a surprise for him
during the season. You know what he did? He smiled. He loved it. He
told me he was looking forward to it.

And you know, my idea was great. It was changing my name from
Johnson to Ochocinco and doing it legally. Man, that was brilliant.
Like I said, I'm a marketing genius. But what does the NFL do when I
come up with that idea? They find a way to stop me. Yeah, they let me
be announced at games as Ochocinco, but they didn't really push it.
They found a way to stop me by not letting me change my jersey. Them
and Reebok.

Here's what happened: I change my name after people have been talking about it all off-season. It's funny and everybody is laughing. Then the league comes in and discourages me, saying that they can't do this to the sponsors, the merchandisers. Then Reebok tells me—and I had my marketing guy, Robert Bailey, talk to Don Hasselbeck from Reebok, who is also the father of Seattle quarterback Matt Hasselbeck—that I can do it if I'm basically willing to let them out of the contract. They owe me $500,000 total for 2008 and 2009, something like that. They say I can make the money back if I play well and sell a bunch of new Ochocinco jerseys, enough to make up the difference in having to recall the Chad Johnson jersey. I'm like, are you kidding me? I'm trying to sell more product for you, find a new way to market myself, and you want me to take the risk, which involves taking a risk on my team? I'm not doing that. Was I right? Of course, Carson gets hurt, we suck, and all of a sudden nobody cares about buying the jerseys.

Look, the NFL is going to market certain individuals, certain players. I'm one of those that they do market for commercials and all that. But I want to take the brand, the Ochocinco brand, that name, and I want to take it to another level. The NFL is going to only do so much. I think of all the things that I can do to take it to that next level. That's why I changed my name, but still the NFL messed with me about changing my name. I knew they were going to find some way to stop me at first, come up with something, but I'll win.

People laugh at me and say, "Oh, he's so crazy." They laugh and they think it's funny, but I know that name change will lead to other opportunities during the off-season. The NFL understands what I'm trying to do. It's going to make them money, so I don't get why they make such a big deal out of it. It's just they want control of everything, and I'm doing something that has never been done before, so of course next year there will be a rule against it. I guarantee it.

The NFL is totally freaked that somebody is going to sell their name as advertising on the back of the jersey, like Michelin Tires. Like Joey Porter or somebody else is going to have "Goodrich" or "Pirelli" on the back of his jersey. Come on, nobody is taking it that far. I'm not even doing that. I'm taking what was my nickname and turning it into my name. I'm promoting me, just like I am if I have "Johnson" on the back of my jersey. It's no different, it's just that my nickname is unique, people recognize me.

Really, the league should allow me to do whatever I want, because the people love it. It's fun and entertaining. If I was in charge of the league, I'd let somebody like me go off. It's good for the league, puts people in the seats. And I'm not selling the name on my jersey to some company. You know why? Because I'm not trying to just sell one product.

I'm selling Ochocinco, the brand.

Now, when Ochocinco really gets going, I'm going to take off with it. Ochocinco Cologne, Ochocinco Sportswear. I'm going to need help from the outside, but I'm going to take that brand and it's just going to be that name. I'm telling you, trust me, watch. It's going to be big. Ochocinco Cigars, straight from Havana. Me and Castro are going to sit there shaking hands. Some folks in Miami might not be happy with that, but it'll be all right. It's Ochocinco. Sunglasses, hats, clothing, shoes, cleats, the whole thing, man. Condoms? Definitely. Stay safe with

Ochocinco. You can't go wrong if you are 85 inches. That would be a great ad.

See, I get it. I get the entertainment part. I get the show. That's why I say I need to be on a winner, because that's where it all starts. Yahoo! came to me that year because everybody still expected the Bengals to be good in 2007. Hell, I did, too. If the Bengals are good and if I'm good, then it all falls into place for me and everybody else.

There's so much out there if you're a winner. Look at Dennis Rodman. Even today he's making serious coin. Why? Because he's some freak? No, because he's some freak who won a lot. Detroit, Chicago, he won championships. Yeah, he wasn't Michael Jordan, but he was damn good. What happened when the Bulls got him? They set a record for wins in a season. He put them over the top to being historic. That's what people want to see, and they love it. They put up with everything when you win like that. The more outrageous, the better.

This is how I am, thinking about ways to market myself and capitalize on who I am. That's what everybody is trying to do out there. And when you put the camera in front of me, you are going to get everything you want and then some. I have a knack for being in front of that camera, it don't matter what it is. I've done TV shows, talk shows, the whole nine yards, everything. You know, you've seen it. When that camera starts rolling, I'm kicking it in gear. It's all natural. I love the camera and it loves me.

One of the things that Yahoo! loved about me was that I was so at ease in front of the camera. You should check me out in the *ESPN The Magazine* shoot I did when I got to be the editor for their "Revenge of the Jocks" issue in 2008. That was the issue where they had a picture of me naked with me holding a copy of a book that has a cover saying, "The Naked Truth According to Chad Johnson." That was hilarious. Hey, take me as I am. The best part is that we have a picture of that with this disclaimer saying: "This is the cover I would have run if *The Magazine* wasn't owned by the fine, family-friendly folks at Disney. You're welcome, Mickey." Then they run it anyway. Just awesome. My grandma flipped out about that. Oh well.

I think that was one of my best ideas yet. The whole message is "Take me as I am." I hear a lot of criticism about the way I am, the way I play, my mouth, I'm arrogant, I'm cocky, this or that. Shut the fuck up, and take me as I am. Actually, I did come into the world naked, and hey, I'm cute just like I was way back then. There are not too many people that can do that and get away with it.

So we did a video to go with it about the making of the magazine. ESPN is interviewing me poolside. They have a guy doing a story about me, filming the whole thing. It's awesome. At one point, I'm talking when they ask me about how I act on the field. I nailed the answer: "Some people call it cocky, some call it arrogant. I call it extravagant. A lot of people want to call me a distraction. I consider myself the attraction."

Come on, man, that's like something straight out of Muhammad Ali in his prime. That's beautiful. Another time, ESPN interviewed me after the league made all these changes to the celebration rules. The NFL Competition Committee basically took everything away. It was bullshit, but whatever. Anyway, ESPN runs my quote: "Of course you cannot stop someone as creative as me. Tell the Competition Committee that

Chad said you can't cover 85 and there's no way you can stop him from entertaining."

Hell, my outtakes from games are awesome—you know, like when they film me before a game or on the sideline. It's not just the celebrations, the touchdown dances. I'm bringing it all the time. Like the time I said before a game, "I'm the mouth, the motor that keeps us going." Or the time we're getting ready to play Jacksonville and I'm supposed to match up with Rashean Mathis. I got on him good. Anyway, I look at the camera and say, " 'Shean Mathis, you know him?" Then I pause just a little and say, "Me neither, mark that on the checklist. Rashean, you can't cover me." I do this stuff off the top of my head. Before another game: "Yeah, it's Ochocinco. It's going to be better than Jones-Tarver 1, 2, and 3. It's going to be better than the Thrilla in Manila."

And there was the time I walked up to the officials before a game and told them, "I got a great celebration for you today." You know I've done all the goofy stuff, the gold teeth, the Mohawk, all that stuff. But man, I'm taking it all to another level. I know how to entertain. I know what people want. I know what gets people excited. Like I said, the league should embrace me. Hell, they shouldn't fine me, they should pay me for coming up with the next great celebration. I'm serious. If my stuff is good enough, I should get an extra check straight from Roger Goodell. Something like $100,000 for the best celebration that week. Just something great.

Now see, the league would probably freak out because all these guys who shouldn't be dancing and celebrating would start doing it. But what we should have is like an *American Idol* or *Dancing with the Stars* competition in the off-season to see which guys get to dance during the regular season. If you don't qualify, you don't get to celebrate. In fact, if you're trash and you try to dance, you should get kicked out of the league for like a week or two. You gotta show that you have something that qualifies to compete for the extra prize.

And seriously, no offensive linemen get to dance. Can't have that, them big ol' bodies moving around that way. That's wrong.

Anyway, this is just the way I am in front of the camera. It's like that first time I stepped on the field for an NFL game. It's just the way I am. I don't know what it is, but when that camera starts running, ding, that's me. I'm ready. I'm going to be there for that. People know it, too. I get calls for reality shows all the time. I've had three different agencies contact me about a reality show. I'll do one of those eventually. I just gotta figure out the right format. At one point, I was going to do this show where I competed against all these athletes in their sport. I'd be embarrassing people in their game left and right.

Now, people think I'm just trying to line it up so I can be on ESPN or CBS or NBC or FOX and do one of the network shows. Man, that's too easy, doing the network stuff, just talking about football. I can do that right now, boom.

What I want to do is act. Yeah, act, like The Rock, action movies, anything. I'm not going to limit myself about what I can play. I'll do the acting lessons. I'll do the work it takes. I'm going to be ready to do it, just like I am in football. I'm serious about my craft and I'm not limiting myself in any way. I'm not just going up there to be clowning around. I see it kind of like Jamie Foxx, how he came up in a comedic way, but then every role he does now is a little different in what you see. He does things now outside the realm of what you think he can do. I can do that, because I'm the same way. I can flip right away, give a different side of my personality right away. I got the idea to do this from watching Denzel Washington. I know that I can do that.

Look, football is great and I love it. I would have loved to play soccer, but I couldn't do that and really make it. I had to choose football. Once I chose football, I mastered it. I'm the best at what I do. But this is not the end of the line for me. I'm not just going to be a football player. I've got bigger drive, bigger ambition. I just want to be the best at what I do and I want to have fun doing it. That makes people think I don't take it serious, but I take it so serious.

That's why acting is so natural for me. Look, I'm already in front of the camera as it is. I just think it's something I would enjoy after football. But I have to start it now. I think the transition will be easy because of my natural ability to flip and do different things in front of the camera.

Once I put my mind to it, I will do it and I will be good.

I've never seen a guy run a comeback route the way he runs it. There's no wasted motion, there's no stutter in his steps, there's nothing that gives away that route, and every receiver in the league other than him gives away that route, somehow. . . . I don't know how to explain it. There's no other receiver that I've seen that can do that. No one can run that route that way, like that. It's only natural to chop [your steps], you have to slow down. I mean, these are the laws of physics. It must come to that, but this guy runs just like that.

—Nnamdi Asomugha, Oakland Raiders Pro Bowl cornerback

ELEVEN

HOW DO YOU PLAY
LIKE ME? YOU CAN'T

SO YOU WANT TO know what the huddle is like? It can get a little crazy, but it's pretty much no-nonsense. My quarterback, Carson Palmer, controls the huddle. He don't play. You get out of line in the huddle, he'll tell you to shut up. He never has to tell me to shut up. He has to tell me all the time to get back in the huddle. I'm always messing with the people up front on the defensive line. Like during a TV time-out, I do all my talking. During the TV time-out, I'm never in the huddle. Then I hear, "Bring your fuckin' ass back here." Something like that. Or me and T. J. [Houshmandzadeh] are fooling around, doing something up front. And don't let us be winning, then it's on. We ain't paying attention to shit in the huddle. My offensive linemen get mad at me all the time because I'll be fuckin' with the defensive linemen, gettin' them all mad, and then my offensive linemen have to deal with it. Willie Anderson, my old teammate who played right tackle, used to tell me to shut up all the time. Levi Jones tells me all the time. It's more, "Don't wake my guy up, I'm the one who has to deal with him." So I leave the defensive linemen alone and start messing with the secondary.

But as far as like demanding the ball, that just goes with the territory if you're a receiver, at least if you're a good receiver. If you're a great receiver like me, you expect the ball all the time. I know I can break down a defense anytime, so give me the ball. And it ain't like it's all polite and I say, "Will you please throw me the ball?" That's not how you ask for the ball. That's not the way you do it. It's like, "Man, let's fucking go." I tell Carson all the time, "You treat me like I'm your insurance. I got you." That's my favorite word, insurance. I tell him all the time, "I got you covered, I'm your man, just give me the ball."

When I'm out there on the field, it's just me and the cornerback. The other 10 guys on defense, they are invisible. I don't even see them. Nobody thinks the way I do out there. Whoever is out there trying to cover me is going to get their ass wore out. People don't understand what I can do. They think I'm so fast or I'm so quick or I can adjust to the ball. Yeah, there's some of all of that. But the reality is that what I do is stuff that most fans can't see or they can't really understand. I'll put it to you another way: You can't touch me. Literally, you can't touch me.

How could you? There's no cornerback or safety or defensive player, period, in the league that can touch me. Doesn't happen, I'm too quick. I shouldn't be like that, because I'm a big receiver. I'm 6-foot-2 and 195 pounds, but I was trained like a guy who is 5-foot-9, 160 pounds. That's all from Charles Collins, who coached me way back at Santa Monica College. He coached me to play like a smaller receiver, because that's how he played. He's a smaller guy, and the moves that he knew were about taking short, quick steps. I have real long legs, like I'm supposed to be a quarter-mile runner, but I run like a small guy. The way I move, I should be in a Broadway show. I'm that good.

Two things will have you lasting forever in the NFL as a receiver, that's all it comes down to. Being able to beat man-to-man and to separate. If you can't separate, you can't get open. That's all it's about, nothing else. It sounds simple, but it's not. It's an art, there's a craft to it. When you master it within your own realm of what you can do, that's when you become successful.

I did it over and over and over for 10 years now. You start off small, five yards, being able to go as fast as possible and transition. Run right in front of you, just go straight and work on it over and over, cutting to the left, cutting to the right. Speed, cutting to the right, speed, cutting to the left. Really, that's all your routes right there. Never rounded off, just doing sharp. If you think about it, that's every route all in one. It's a curl, it's out, either way you put it, it's a slant, it's every route all in one. Cones, cones, cones, then comes being able to beat man-to-man. You get your feet and the hips right, then Coach C began to teach me the ability to beat man-to-man, being able to understand technique and know what he's going to do before he even does it. All the hand movement, watching his feet, understanding leverage, what he's trying to do, what he doesn't want you to do. Just little stuff like that just makes a difference. On that stuff, I'm just a sponge, big-time. If I was like that in school, I would have been a genius.

Now, my ability to adjust to the ball in the air, that's easy. That's a natural thing. You don't teach that, that's natural. There are certain things you can't teach, like fucking. You can't teach somebody how to fuck. You have to do it enough to where it's natural. Bitch, ain't no class on that shit. Ain't no class on how to adjust on the ball, that's a natural gift. Every running back can't run the ball. Every running back can't make certain moves, do you know what I mean?

I practiced and practiced for three years in junior college and it all started to come together at Oregon State. I came to Cincinnati, but it still wasn't as crisp, but it was good. It was good enough to the point if you were to see me and knew how Coach C coached me, you could tell right away what I had worked on.

I am exceptionally good at getting open, there is no excuse and I don't make any. I like to put all my coaches in the comfort zone like that. I'm way better than AIG these days. I'm Marvin's best insurance. I'm no different. That's the level of confidence that I'll play with week in and week out, even when we're getting our ass whupped. I'm not as vocal about it, but nothing has changed. Let somebody give you our game film, just any game film from this year. We're getting our ass whupped, and look at me on film. You would swear I'm playing for the Super Bowl.

Ask guys around the league and they'll tell you. Cornerbacks try to bump me all the time, but they can't get their hands on me. They miss and I'm gone. That's why they're so scared. Don't believe me? Ask my offensive coordinator, Bob Bratkowski: "I've had coaches from other teams say it. They're scared to death of him and their corners are scared to death of him. You don't get that reaction in this league very much. There are only a couple of players who are like that."

Or there's New York Jets coach Rex Ryan, who I faced all the time when he was defensive coordinator in Baltimore: "Chad's ability to adjust his body along the sideline and when the ball is in the air is phenomenal. There's nobody like him in the league. Nobody even close when it comes to body control."

It's like what Nnamdi Asomugha was talking about to start this chapter. You can try anything, but I'm going to get open. That's because I can run as fast through my cuts as I do running straight ahead, full speed. I don't have to slow down, because of the way I was trained. I'm serious. Go try it. Go out in the street or in your yard or go down to the school around the corner and try it. Try running as fast as you can and turn right or left at full speed. You're either going to slow down or you're going to fall. Bring some Band-Aids, just in case.

THE CHAD TESTIMONIALS

Chad is one of the most difficult guys I've had to cover. I know we were playing on his turf and I know he's a lot better on turf than on grass, like everyone. I don't know how he is on grass. But I'll tell this to anyone who asks me. I tell them how great Randy Moss is and I had to practice against Randy all the time. They ask about Chad and I say, I've never seen a guy run routes like that. Really, there's just no wasted motion. He's incredible. He makes one move and he's gone. When he runs the comeback route, it's not even really a comeback, because he can just stop, boom, like that, and he's done. If you don't anticipate it, you have to give it to him. There are receivers in this league that you, the cornerback, can make a great play against even if you weren't expecting that route, because those receivers will give it away. They don't sell it well. They give away what they're going to do with how they run, how they change speed or cut or stop. You can figure most guys out pretty fast. With Chad, I had never seen anything like that before. I couldn't figure it out. I would press him, I played off on him. I played off on him one time and they hit a post when my safety left me and he caught like a 35-yard pass.

—**Nnamdi Asomugha,** Oakland Raiders Pro Bowl cornerback

You have to take him seriously and be careful with him on every play because he's one of the best receivers in the game. His ability to cut at full speed is unreal. He could probably tell you what he was running before the route and still fool you because of his cuts. He's one of the best at doing that, especially playing on that surface that they have, that fast surface. It makes his cutting ability and coming out of his breaks just as fast. He's one of the best at showing the same thing on every route. He can show a quick tempo, get in and out of his breaks, and run that same way when you're running a deep nine [fly] route with him and he just takes off.

—**Brian Dawkins,** Denver Broncos Pro Bowl safety

He's out of this world. I tell people, he has two types of speed. He has fast and faster, and most guys in this league are already fast, but he happens to be faster. His body control running in and out of routes is unbelievable. Truly special. You have that and then the fact that he's so confident, so willing to tell you the whole time what he's going to do to you, man, it can be scary if you let it get in your head. I like to be feisty with him, because that's just how I have to play. I can't back down. But I know plenty of guys, they don't want to get up there and bump with him because they know they might miss. His footwork is unreal.

—**Cortland Finnegan,** Tennessee Titans
Pro Bowl cornerback

He's one of the top route runners in the game. He's a great route runner. A lot of people think he's super fast. He's fast, but he's not super fast. He's quick and controls his body so well that it makes you think he's faster than he is.

—**Al Harris,** Green Bay Packers Pro Bowl cornerback

See, I told you. People talk about Randy Moss and Marvin Harrison and Terrell Owens all the time. Hey, those guys are damn good. I'm not taking any of those guys down. T. O. is a good dude and a great player. His personality is nothing like what people say it is, all disruptive or whatever people think. But if you want to talk about playing, I think I'm the best. That's just how it is. I know what I can do on that goddamn field and I know I can't be stopped. You can put the best cornerback in the league out there in front of me and I can't be stopped. Some guys say, "Oh, put a backup in front of me, and I'm thinking this dude is lunch." Man, you put a starter in front of me and I'm thinking he's dinner.

And like I said, I'm going to tell anybody and everybody what I think. I'm not afraid, I'm not backing down. As I said before a game once, I was staring right into the camera and said: "I got a trivia question. It's a new year with the same old question. How do you stop 85?" You can't. I'm going to get you. And it's not just the running ability. Look at the stuff I do around the sideline or stuff that I do when I'm in the air and adjust to the ball. We had this one game against Pittsburgh. I was on the right side and I ran an out route on the sideline. Carson fires the ball low and out of bounds. When you watch the tape of the game and listen to the announcer, he's kind of nonchalant, like he thinks it's going to be incomplete. He's just talking and says, "To Chad Johnson . . . He caught that? Oh my." I mean, he was totally shocked, like what the fuck did I just see? That was cool.

Or there was the time Carson hit me with like a 50-yard throw against Baltimore cornerback Chris McAlister. The ball is a little short and I have to find a way to slow my body down. I gather myself just a little, jump, turn my body in the air, and then grab the ball right off the top of McAlister's helmet. Oh man, he was pissed. I fall down after the catch. You can see McAlister get up and look for the ball as the safety runs over and touches me before I can get up.

The fact is, when I'm in the game, we run different stuff. You can't run the stuff we do with me with other guys. I'm not saying that to be cocky or put down our other guys. We have some guys who are great. T. J. Houshmandzadeh is great. I'm going to miss him, and I can tell you, he does stuff I can't do. If I played like him, I'd end up in the hospital. We got guys like Chris Henry. He's going to be awesome when he settles down and gets himself straight. We got some other young guys. We got Laveranues Coles now, who's a tough guy, another dude from Florida. But when I say that the other guys don't run the routes the same way I do, I mean it. They don't. They can't. As I said before, ask the coaches.

BOB **BRATKOWSKI**
Cincinnati Bengals offensive coordinator

Chad has the ability to do things that are rare. The ability to stop is obvious. His ability to keep his feet on the sideline and catch a ball that's two and a half or three yards out of bounds is freakish. That's the only way I can describe it. He's able to fully extend his body while keeping his toes right on the line, extend his arms, and then pick off the ball. He's absolutely special with that ability to stretch and change his body. He's basically elastic. In the coaches' meeting during the week, we have called him Gumby. We'll be looking at plays he makes and he looks like Gumby the way he moves around. His ability to stop, alter his body, it's a combination of rhythm, flexibility, quick-twitch muscle movement. That's the best way to describe it. Yes, without a doubt, he has an explosiveness and suddenness that you don't have very much, even in this sport. It's very similar to ballet, the speed and suddenness, but you're talking about doing that with a 6-foot-2, 195-pound man who is wearing shoulder pads, a helmet, and the rest of that uniform.

He can run routes against any type of cornerback, big, small, a technician, a physical guy. The biggest thing is if he can get a cornerback running one way, he has that guy set up, because then he can just stop his body and go a different direction. You see it so many times. The cornerback is moving and you see them look back to find Chad and their reaction is like, "Where did he go?" You teach pretty much the same plays to everybody. It's not like you can have a separate set of plays, but there are certain plays we only run with Chad. We have other wide receivers who we try to teach how to run it. You try to teach it, but it's hard for them to learn it. They really have to observe it, see what it's supposed to be like, and then they try it. But they don't have the ability to run certain plays versus certain defensive backs that Chad can run. Really, the best way to put it is there are things we do only with him. If we're going against a certain defender and Chad isn't out there, we tell the quarterback just look the other way.

How he reacts to the ball in the air, if it's high or behind him, his ability to go one direction and bend his body back, lean back, pirouette back and catch the ball . . . some of what he can do when he's in the air, you just can't teach. There are certain things he's not good at. Going across the middle in traffic, he doesn't like that, and he's too anxious at this point in his career to run double moves, like a down-out-and-up. He doesn't see the need for it, because his first move is so good. He looks at you and says, "Why do I need to make a second move?" But if you get him in any one-on-one situation, running a shallow crossing route or a deep over route, he's just amazing with his ability to get open. He has a rare combination of ability. Joey Galloway, early in his career, had the rare ability to go against bump-and-run coverage and completely avoid the bump, and he could stop like Chad. When I was in Pittsburgh, I had Hines Ward. He's completely different, but both have the passion for the game. I had Plaxico

Burress in Pittsburgh, and he has such grace and athletic ability for his size. But Chad is different in his package of skills.

HUE JACKSON
former Cincinnati Bengals wide receivers coach

You want to understand his skills? There's probably six guys, at the most, at any given time in the league who have anything like his body control. Now, I'm just talking about the body control. I'm not talking about the ability to catch it, to adjust in the air, to track a ball. I mean, there are catches he makes where he completely turns around and finds the ball again. He can take his eyes off the ball completely and find it after he turns. Put all those together and you have Chad. But the body control alone is fascinating. It's ridiculous, especially for a man his size. To me, the thing I want to see is him go on that *Dancing with the Stars* program one year. You see guys like Emmitt Smith and Jason Taylor and Warren Sapp and you think, "Man, those guys are amazing." But they have nothing on Chad. He would look like one of the professionals, his feet are that good and his body control is that good.

So are you getting it now? You understand what I do, how I change a game? My ability is sick. When I get out there, it's not a question of whether I'm confident or not, it's about how confident I am. That's why the huddle can be so crazy sometimes. Look, I know if they get me the ball, something great is going to happen. I just *know* it. Now, my coach, Marvin Lewis, is always getting on me about being there in the off-season and practicing and all that. He was trying to tell me that part of the problem last season was that my timing was off. That's not what it was. The problem last season is that Carson got hurt, we started losing, and they didn't throw me the ball. I truly believe they were making me pay my penance. What else am I supposed to think? I'm still me, running wide open all over the field.

Yeah, yeah, that don't make sense. I hear that from Bratkowski. He told me over and over, "Chad, do you really think at this level that coaches are going to do things that don't help them win games? Do you really think we're going to take a chance with our futures like that? Do you really think all we're trying to do is teach you a lesson?" I hear that, but I'm still running down the field, waving my arms because I'm wide open. Like I said, look at the tape of the games, you'll see it. It's not about all that stuff and it's not about what Marvin is saying about timing. I mean, really, you think it's all about timing? When you have a quarterback like Carson Palmer, it's not about timing. We can get that stuff down in a few days of practice. That's not it. It shouldn't take long. I don't care if we miss months, we should be able to do it with our eyes closed. I don't care what nobody says. We put too much on that. It's like with Peyton Manning and Marvin Harrison the last couple of years. When they got back out there, they had their timing down right away. They didn't have a problem. Speaking of that, what I wouldn't give to be in that offense. Man, to be with a quarterback who has all that freedom to pass as much as he wants. We're still about making the running game go all the time, because that's how our division works. In Indy, they don't care. Same in New

England, all they want to do is move the ball however they do it. I'd give all my paychecks to play in something like that.

Now, I admit, as I said before, I get distracted about some things on the field. Hey, man, I'm trying to stay amped up, keep the guy I'm playing against playing hard so I feel challenged. I have to do stuff like that. I have to be on edge. It's like the story about the $100,000 check I gave to the coaches to keep if I didn't play well the rest of the season. I was looking for a way to challenge myself, to stay on top of my game. I have to do that stuff. That's the game for me. If I have to do it in the middle of a game, I have to do it. Brat gets on me about that sometimes, but me and Carson have it worked out. Brat will tell me, "You missed this call in the huddle and such and such because you're talking too much." He thinks I'll be late picking up the audible if Carson is trying to change things. But Carson knows how to get my attention and it doesn't take much. All we really have to do at this point is make eye contact and make sure we got it. Sometimes Brat gets on me when we run no-huddle because I'm slow to get back to the line and maybe I'm talking shit to some defensive back. Hey, whatever, you know what it's about with the defensive backs and me.

I don't have any of those pregame rituals or anything, like having to listen to certain music or get taped up a certain way. I'm not keyed up at all. I don't say anything. I'm quiet. I don't say a word, listen to my headphones. Then I just go out. Now, when I touch the ball, you can see the energy just—it's something about getting the ball. I don't know what it is, I swear to God. As soon as I touch it, it just revives me. I don't know what word to use. You can ask Coach Lewis. You got to get me involved early. It's not about throwing the ball deep or none of that. Just put the ball in my hands any way. When I touch that ball, I am set for four quarters. I am ready to go. I don't know what it is, I don't know why I'm like that. It's like my mojo and it gets me going.

It's like when some guys talk about getting hit the first time in the game. You know how you get butterflies before the game, you're nervous? I think for a defensive player or a running back when you get that first hit, it relaxes you. Now you are ready to play. When I touch that ball, it relaxes me and it's like, "Hurry up, I want it, I want it." It relaxes me. Now, when I get frustrated is when the motherfucker doesn't come and you know what it takes to get me involved in the game and keep me going. That's when I get pissed the fuck off. That's what happened at that Pittsburgh game at halftime, I went through a whole half and they let me have one ball. This is one of the biggest games, and the Bengals are allowing the Steelers to dictate what you want to do with me.

I hear the stories about Jerry Rice, how he had to have his uniform just a certain way and he'd be looking in the mirror, make sure his shit was just perfect, that he looked good. That's cool, that's his thing, and hey, you can't argue with it. He's probably the greatest player of all time. Not greatest *receiver*, greatest *player*. Yeah, yeah, I hear all that about Jim Brown being the greatest of all time. I've seen some of his stuff on TV, the old films and stuff. Jim Brown was a beast running out there. But come on now, he was running against dudes who weren't like they are now. He was bigger than some of the linemen. The game is different now. It's a wide receivers' game. So we gotta keep the Jim Brown–Jerry Rice thing in some perspective. Otherwise, it sounds like the barbershop scene from *Coming to America*. That movie is a classic. Absolute classic. Eddie Murphy is a fucking genius, probably the funniest dude ever. Yeah, I don't know about Richard Pryor. Kind of before my time. I heard he did some outrageous stuff onstage, but his movies are just OK. Not like *Coming to America*. Yeah, Chris Rock is good, but he's more political. I mean, come on, watch *Raw* or *Delirious* with Eddie and you'll see what I mean.

That's what I'm saying about Jerry Rice. You just have to look at him and put in perspective what he did. He has the numbers, he won the titles, he has everything. That's what I want to be by the time I'm done. I want the titles, the records, everything. That's what any player wants.

Anyway, we were talking about rituals and I don't have to do anything weird. I don't have to drive the same way to the game every time or get my ankles wrapped a certain way or have a certain meal before the game. None of that stuff. My uniform, I could really care less, because I know at some point I'm going to get tackled or whatever and that's going to get tossed around. The only thing that I'm very anal about is my shoes and my gloves. They've got to be flashy, orange or black-and-orange, and the bottoms have to be shiny. Reebok makes a certain shoe and glove just for me. The bottoms are like metallic shiny because it just looks cool when I'm running. I have one with a chrome bottom and the other with a metallic orange bottom, both really shiny. Reebok came up with that, and I really like it. They sent me stuff they thought I'd like and that's one that's really good. When I'm running, that looks nice. My gloves also have to match my shoes. Yeah, just the color combination, that's all. Like a woman's purse and her shoes. Purse and shoes have got to go together. For me, it's the gloves and the shoes. Other than that, I couldn't really care less.

But I really don't have any routines. As far as music, I just listen to whatever. Whatever I click on I just listen to it. My whole thing, and I wouldn't call it a routine, it's just something everybody does, is you go out and warm up with the quarterback and that's it. We throw maybe five routes, pass deep, talk real quick about what we have today and what he might want to throw. That's about it. Real simple. My whole thing is real simple. Yeah, some guys have to get in like a trance or some shit. Some guys have the headphones on and they're going somewhere else in their mind. They're bobbing their head to rap music or whatever. The locker room isn't real loud before games. Guys are talking, but the music doesn't get like all loud, because everybody kind of has their own music, if that's what they do.

Now, during the week, when I come in early, I'll put on music and I'm all over the place. Jazz, big band, classical, metal, whatever. I can't listen to the same stuff every day. Like T. J., the only thing he listens to is rap. That's it. If I'm playing music, he comes in and is like, "What the hell is this?" He starts complaining about all the stuff I play. I just laugh.

But before a game, that's different. Some guys are focusing, doing what they have to do, whatever. I don't pay anybody else any attention, because I'm always in my own zone. They can do all that, man, but it's all football. It all comes down to what you do on the field. It's not about rituals and all that stuff. It has nothing to do with all that. It's about using your technique to the best of your abilities in that three seconds of the play. That's it. If you're focused on that, you'll be fine.

And, as I said, I'm focused. I'm focused from like Friday night. I've been thinking about the game all week. Like I said before, I'm thinking about the game on Tuesday, Wednesday, and Thursday. I'm calling my coaches at like three in the morning with ideas. The first time I did that with Brat, he got all freaked out. He thought something serious had happened, that I was in trouble. Come on, this is Chad. I don't do stupid stuff like get arrested. I don't smoke, I don't drink, I don't do drugs. I've never been arrested in the NFL. That's not happening. Could you imagine what would happen if that did happen? Oh shit, everybody would be on my ass, saying, "I told you so, I told you so."

Anyway, I've called Brat in the middle of the night. Woke his ass up to tell him what's going on. To me, that's funny. Their wives might not like it, but I don't care. They got to deal with that, not me. Hey, during football season, he's mine. That's what I would tell her.

BOB BRATKOWSKI
Cincinnati Bengals offensive coordinator

Yeah, I've had those calls. Some, I've answered. Some, I just look at the phone and look at the clock and think, "Chad, whatever it is, it can wait until the morning." I'm just thinking, "Why don't you write it down and go to bed and we'll talk about it later." He should just keep a little notepad by the bed so he can write down his ideas. Sometimes, it's really not even an idea. He calls me and says, "I'm just so excited about the game." OK, Chad, that's nice. Can I get some sleep? The first couple of times he called, you're thinking, "Oh my God, what happened? Is he OK? What's the emergency?" It's like with your kids.

You worry that you're going to get that call in the middle of the night when they're out. But after the first couple, I kind of got the idea what was going on. My wife is patient with it. She knows all about Chad, and I say that in a good way. She likes him. My kids like him. They've known him the whole time we've been here and he's been here. He's a charming, earnest guy. Yeah, he's changed since he got here, but he's still the guy who is passionate about the game. He truly loves the game, everything about it.

He still listens, for the most part. But I think his own drumbeat is overriding things a little bit more now. When he first got here, he was Chad Johnson. Then he became Ochocinco and that alter ego has taken over a little bit. I don't talk to Ochocinco. I talk to Chad or C. J. But the guy who I talk to, regardless, is a special talent. He's absolutely unique.

You have women who come right up to him, anytime, anyplace, and you can see what they want. It ain't no secret, but it's ridiculous. How do you handle that if you're in his position? I know how most guys would be, and that's what happens to athletes, that's why so many guys have problems. They can't say no. It's taken Chad a while to figure out who he can trust and who he can't. But I can tell you this, trusting any woman if you're an athlete has got to be like impossible.

—**Bo Johnson,** Chad Ochocinco's half brother

TWELVE

WOMEN

DEALING WITH WOMEN WHEN you get to the NFL, man, it ain't easy. You get all this money, and you have all these women at your disposal. At some point, I think it's a phase or a stage you go through when you are going to have fun. You're going to do your thing, trust me. You're going to do it, and you're going to meet all types of women, and it's just about being careful and watching yourself.

You gotta be careful. You gotta think about who you're going to be with. It's coming at you from all different type of ways. It's hard, it's really hard to be in a relationship and traveling all the time, seeing different women. And there's something about the temptation, you have to be strong. For those men who are able to do it, to deal with one person, to deal with one person all the time consistently, I don't know how they do it. There's something about seeing another woman that's beautiful, seeing those things that you like and seeing the things you like in her as a person, all of a sudden it's "Man, I wonder what that's like?"

The way I describe it to women about why men are the way they are, I always tell women, "Think about when you go to the mall and you see that Louis [Vuitton] purse or those Louis shoes, that Gucci bag or those Gucci shoes, or maybe some nice jewelry, that feeling that a woman has as soon as she sees it and you've got to have it." That's how it is for men. It's similar. That's the only example I can think of that explains how we think. But the shoes and the purse thing . . . you know how women are with that stuff. For a man, there's something about a new woman, it's refreshing or something.

I don't know if it goes away, but all ages seem to have the same problem. Women say a man will grow out of it, it's a phase. Well, it ain't no phase, because you have politicians, governors, going through it. Look at the dude up in New York, the governor and the hooker. Presidents get in trouble. We're talking about different realms of life, from rich people to middle class to everybody. It has nothing to do with age or how much money you have or what you do. It has to do with being a man. It's just the way it is, and when dealing with us high-profile athletes, it takes a very strong woman to understand there are going to be things you have to deal with. It's not always going to be peaches and cream. The thing about most successful relationships for professional athletes is that the woman was there before the guys were who they are. That's what I think. Anyone you meet at this point, when you're in the league, it is so hard for us to tell the difference. Is she with me for me, or is she with me because of what I do or because of the money? Whatever it is.

The worst thing for women is that they drive themselves crazy. So many women chase athletes, chase them even when they know that guy has a girlfriend or even a wife. These women don't care, they're just going after what they want. Hey, I understand that motivation. Like I said, people see things they want and they go after them. But the crazy thing is that after women get involved with guys, maybe steal the guy away from his girlfriend or wife, what does the new woman do? She gets jealous. She gets controlling and angry and frustrated. I mean, what did you think was going to happen? You go after this guy, expect he's going to chase you, but then he's not going to chase the next person who does the same thing as you? Come on, ladies, think about it.

That brings me to my story about my craziest girlfriend. It was about three years ago. Somehow, she set it up so she got all my text messages from all my phones. She was a computer whiz, so she set it up to get all my messages I was sending to or getting from other girls, doing whatever I was doing. Every time I was out doing something with some other woman, she'd call me right after and say, "Where've you been?" It was like crazy. I couldn't figure it out.

So as we're going along, she's getting more and more tense and I'm getting tense, too. Finally, one day, I was like, "What's going on with you that you're so tense?" She says, "This is why I'm so tense" and she starts reading all my messages I've been sending back and forth with these other women. Yeah, she busted me, but that wasn't ever going to work. Hey, I told her how it was from the start. I was honest about who I am and what I was doing. Just look at my life. Again, you want to get involved with me, but you don't want to understand the deal.

Now, I'm not trying to sell you any line about how I've always been the guy every woman chased. Before I was in the league, I was chasing women just like any other guy. Yeah, I was an athlete and that helped, but I didn't have any money, and no real way to keep women interested in me. I was like so many guys, trying to get all these women, and, yeah, I would go crazy when it didn't go right.

And one time it got bad and I had to learn to control it.

The craziest I've ever been was with this one woman I was dating when I was going to junior college and living in Los Angeles. I was in way over my head. I was nowhere near being in her league and I knew it. She was amazing looking and I didn't have the money to take care of her. I couldn't support her, so I just knew she was going to end up with some other guys. It drove me crazy.

One day, I'm calling her and she's not calling back. I'm calling and calling and she's not picking up and I'm thinking she's out with some other guy or whatever. So I'm going crazy with this shit. She usually would come pick me up from school and give me a ride back to the other side of town. But she didn't show up that day and I'm like, "Where the hell are you?"

Anyway, this is going on for hours and hours and it's messing with my mind. I'm getting more and more freaked out. So finally, in the middle of the night, I run all the way to her house. She lived over by Dorsey High in Los Angeles, and when I get there, I don't see her car. She parked it farther in her garage than usual. So I break into her house through a window and I walk around, when I finally see her.

She's in bed, totally asleep, by herself. So I just get a chair and sit in the middle of the room. She finally wakes up, sees me, and yells at me, "What the hell are you doing here?" I'm like, "What the hell is going on that you don't call me all day?" It gets into this argument, and that's when I put my hands on her and got a DV [domestic-violence violation]. That DV stayed with me all the way to the NFL draft. It was just stupid, because I didn't know how to handle it. I didn't know how to control my emotions when I was in a situation like that, in over my head like that.

Right then and there, I knew there was going to be no more of that. None. I had to get control of my emotions, how I deal with a situation. For me, it takes a lot to get attached to someone if I don't trust them. The lucky part for me is that I'm in a relationship like that now, where I can trust the woman I'm with, that she's not there just for my money or fame or whatever.

It was February 2008, I was in New Orleans for the NBA All-Star Game, and I saw her in the street. That's when I lucked out and met Maya. I was walking down the street in New Orleans and I saw her. Immediately I'm like, I want to talk to this woman, I want to meet her and go out. Most women, it doesn't take long to get their attention, especially after I say my name and tell them I play football. But she ignored me, totally ignored me, kept on walking, shot me down.

Then she happened to be on my flight leaving two days later. It was a Southwest flight back to Miami, so I just grabbed the seat next to her. I talked so much shit. "Just come take over, I'll give you a key, the whole nine yards." Man, she was so bad when I first met her, and I knew, this is the one. I asked her to come stay the night. "I'm not trying anything, I just want you here, blah, blah, blah." She actually came over after the flight, and she has not left my side since then. Every day.

The way I know that Maya is not after something else is because she can take care of herself. She has her own money. That's why I'm never going to find that anywhere else and why she's never going anywhere. I'm never going to find that again. That's luck. I'm not going to fuckin' lie, that's luck. It's a little bit of an uncomfortable feeling for me that she can take care of herself, but I think about what would I have to deal with in some of the others that are chasing me? The ones with intentions, bad intentions at that. It feels very comfortable to have someone on my side who is actually with me because she wants to be with me for just me. Forget football, forget all that. A lot of people ask me, "How the hell did you get her?" Everybody thinks about, "Oh, you're Chad Ochocinco with the gold teeth and the Mohawk." They don't know I'm nothing like that. Maya sees the real Chad, the Chad that nobody else sees, funny, personality, cool as hell. The side nobody else gets to see.

Most relationships I've had, the longest has been about four years or better, so this one is still pretty new. I've been in five serious relationships since I was 19. But this is different because she's different. I really chased her, and she didn't care. She has a pretty strong family. She didn't care about who I was, at all. She couldn't care less. I chased her for so fucking long, she didn't give a fuck who Chad Ochocinco was. You should see how she looked at me when we first met. I said, "How you doing? I'm Chad." She looks at me and says, "Your point?" and walked away. That's never happened to me. Remember, it's usually the other way around. I told myself, once I get her, I'm done.

She's kind of got me in line, 'cause she doesn't need to be with me. I've never been married, but I know this is my last stop. She did it without even forcing the issue. It's just something about being with her just makes me want to do right, I don't know why. It's a very funny feeling.

When you get to the NFL, it's hard to trust a lot of people, especially women. Eventually, you can weed them out, though. At some point, it's going to give in, what she wants, why she's around you. For me, I have to have someone who's equal to me, doesn't just treat me like they're some groupie. You get that all the time.

Like, for instance, Maya doesn't know anything about football. I'm not sure if it's a positive or a negative, but it's different. Usually the women who come around are the ones who know everything about your career, what you do, how you play, and they are always at you for the wrong reasons. But in this case, there is no reason for her to be with me. She doesn't worship me or anything. At least I know that our thing is genuine, what we have. It ain't about football, it's real, and I don't have to sit and wait to see who the real Maya is. The real Maya was there from the beginning, like, "I couldn't care less about who you are, care less about what you have, because I don't need you."

Now, that's unique, totally different. I don't know any other athlete who can say, "Hey, my girl can take care of herself." And as I said, I'm not sure how many guys would be totally comfortable with that. Sure, you might joke around and say, "Cool, I got a sugar momma," but I don't think too many guys would be real cool with it. It's probably about pride, feeling like, "Hey, I'm the man in this relationship." At the same time, you want to feel that way, but that's exactly the stuff that gets you in trouble if you pick the wrong woman.

Guys want to be in control, especially us athletes. That's what we're all about, getting control of a relationship, feeling like we're in charge. I realized that way back when I got in trouble back in junior college with that woman in Los Angeles. I got freaked out because this woman wasn't paying attention to what I wanted. I had to learn to let that go right away or I might not be in the league today.

Now, as far as married life, I talk sometimes about Maya being my wife. We're still getting there, working it out. But from what I've seen, there aren't a lot of marriages for athletes that make me say, "Yeah, that's a good one." My ex-teammate and buddy T. J. Houshmandzadeh has got it down. I say it all the time to myself, he has it right. I don't know how he does it. Every day since junior college, him and his wife, Kaci, their two daughters, Kennedi and Karrington, have been together all the time, consistently. They always seem happy to me. Now, everybody has their ups and downs in their relationships, but they've been plugging away for a while and they always seem just perfect.

Aside from them, out of the married people I surround myself with, there is Coach C [Charles Collins] from my days back at Santa Monica College. He is the only other one who has it down. His wife and him have been together forever and they seem like they have a perfect relationship. I met C in '97, and they've been going strong since long before that.

T. J. and Coach C, those are really the only two people I know who I can say that their marriages are solid, because I've been around them long enough to watch them and know. I've seen how it's been. And what really works for them is that these women, they've been with these guys since before they were anything. T. J. was walking around Oregon State, no money, no car, no nothing, and Kaci was there. There was no assurance he was going to get here, especially back in junior college when

T. J. was a troublemaker and all the stuff he did, all the things he was thinking about.

You see other guys in this league, it's just crazy. Now, I'm not in anybody's business and I don't give advice. Who the fuck am I to give advice? I mean, seriously, what can I tell a guy about handling his relationships? Hey, don't do what I did? Come on, that's not advice. I don't give advice, because whoever it is is going to handle it his own way. To each his own. Every guy is going to handle women in different ways, and I ain't the one to be giving no goddamn advice, because I ain't going to listen to nobody. So I know they ain't going to listen to me. I never listened to anyone, ever, especially about THAT. I will do whatever I want to do.

But the thing that you see so many guys get into is writing checks. Everybody writes checks to take care of the women they have, or their kids, or both. The thing is that some guys are really trying to do it right. They want to have their kids around and be a good dad, but they end up fighting with the woman about something and it's ugly. Or the guy is nervous all the time because he might get cut, and then what's going to happen? Me, I'm lucky, I made it big, I can take care of my kids, and I have a pretty good relationship with the moms. But I've written checks. Sometimes you get in that situation where people are asking you for money and it's your responsibility. You have to provide. Sometimes people ask for more than they should, so you have to deal with those people and move on. That's the way it goes.

But some dudes are crazy, too. I mean, look at Travis Henry. He had nine kids with nine different women, and then I heard he had twins with another woman. I mean, OK, I can see how maybe a guy can say he got trapped by a woman once or twice, had a kid when she said she was on the Pill or something. It's like Ray Lewis told me one time, when you're at that point, you ain't thinking anymore. She tells you she's covered and, hey, you're going to believe it. Probably a couple times, at least.

But 11 kids with 10 women? Come on, man. I'm not saying a guy can't do that if he wants to really have kids, but that's gettin' crazy. Really, that's ridiculous. I mean, come on, wrap that thing up, get the vasectomy, do something, man. And the worst part is that Travis is doing this while he's not even playing. He gets in trouble with the league for the drug policy, gets suspended, gets arrested for dealing drugs or something like that, gets behind on the child support, and they throw his ass in jail. This is how it can all get out of control real fast.

How is he ever going to have a career? You're just throwing it away, and for what? If you get past a few years in this league, you have to learn what the heck is going on, because if you let it get out of control, it's going to end your career.

And this is what plays with your mind as an athlete, as anybody who has something that somebody else wants. That's why it's hard for me to trust anybody. I mean anybody. People come up to you and ask you for anything. Women think they can get it with their bodies.

For me, I have four or five people I really trust. There's Maya, and, I'm telling you, she's different. She's in a whole different world how I can trust her. After her, there's my grandma and four or five guys that I grew up with. That's it. That's probably all there's ever going to be. Seriously, why do I need anybody else to trust? Those are the people I keep around me and lean on. Those are the ones who were there before I was anything, before I had anything to give anybody, and they're the ones who supported me.

Now, when I meet people, there's always some angle. Somebody is trying to sell you something or trying to get you to invest in something, trying to get this or get that or get anything they can. I try to be nice to guys that I grew up with, but I can't help everybody. I help my family, but even with them I say, "Hey, do something to take care of yourself." Don't just sit around living off of me.

Ask my brother Bo. He's a year older than me. Back when I was struggling on the West Coast, going to Santa Monica College or then going up to Oregon State, he helped me out. He sent me money. He was working back home. He was hustling, doin' what he had to do. But he made sure I was all right. So I trust him, and now I help him.

He talks about how funny it is that that's changed, but he also works hard. He works out. He's ripped in his shoulders, strong as hell. He's loud and funny (I can't imagine where he gets that). But he'll tell you what I say to him and our brothers. Do something. Pick up some of the bills. Bo does, no question. Sam does, too. But I'll get more into that later.

But what I see so much of is people trying to hitch a ride on me or some other athlete. It can hurt, if you let it. That's why I say, you have to be careful about the kind of women you are dealing with—you know, the ones that might be trying to set you up. You never know their angle. Every time you deal with someone that you don't have a serious commitment with, it's a gamble. Because all it takes is for her to make one phone call, "Oh, he raped me, he did this, he did that." Your career is really over after that.

Or there are women who want to have a kid with you and get taken care of, and the stuff that women tell you, I wouldn't really consider it being wild. It was just ordinary, everyday shit after a while. "I'll do anything" is not wild, especially with some of the shit I go through or some of the shit I've seen, it's just normal. You get anything at any time. Women walk up to you in the middle of the street and say what they want to do right in your ear. I just shake my head sometimes. I've had it happen to me on Miami Beach. There are women who tell you they'll do you right there on the street in the middle of the day. She wouldn't care who was looking. She just figured that was the way to get to you.

How are you going to trust somebody who has no shame?

He started off playing soccer? Are you serious? Well, I could see that, but I would have thought basketball. Well, I would have thought anything. Baseball, basketball, track, soccer, ice skating . . . anything Chad wants to do, he could do. He's that talented. Like I said before, he could have done ballet, his feet are so good. That's why we call him "The Ballerina" just to mess with him. He's nimble and he doesn't like to be touched.

—**Cortland Finnegan,** Tennessee Titans
Pro Bowl cornerback

THIRTEEN

KING OF ALL SPORTS

WELCOME TO SOUTH BEACH, where I'm hanging out this off-season. This is about 10 miles from where I grew up in Liberty City, but a million miles from that reality. Hell, it's a place where you can find some unreality, like some pretty hot-looking women who are actually dudes. South Beach is beautiful, women walking around in bikinis, if even that. The weather is beautiful, one restaurant after another with open-air seating, kind of like being in Paris or Rome. People-watching, man, I love this. And after doing that one Saturday afternoon in March, I walked two blocks from Ocean Drive to Washington Street, gave up the people-watching for something challenging.

Boxing.

Yeah, boxing. I'm serious. I'm training to be a boxer. People think this shit is a big joke, but I'm in the ring working out with Kevin Kelley, a former two-time world featherweight champion. He's all of

5-foot-8, but quick as hell, and he's showing me the ropes, literally. You want to know how serious I am about this? I'm spending two hours at South Florida Boxing & Fitness with Kelley, twice a day. And this ain't no pretty-boy L.A. Fitness place with all those clean machines. This is a real gym. Cinder-block walls, pipes showing in the ceiling, tiny windows for just enough ventilation, but not enough to keep it cool. The only air-conditioning is some ceiling fans. If you didn't know better, this would just be some warehouse to store stuff. There's a mixed martial arts cage, a boxing ring right next to that, and 38 big weight bags hanging from the ceiling. (It's actually a little spooky; this could be the set for another remake of *Invasion of the Body Snatchers,* with all the bags hanging there.) There's some weight machines, but nothing really fancy. This is what it's all about. This is what I want to do.

And Kelley is drilling me. Not like with his fists. We ain't punching for real, just learning how to do it, how to react, how to handle punches, how to avoid them, how to deliver them and deliver them with power. We start off with him taking a rope and taking it across the ring, cutting the boxing ring diagonally into two triangles. My job is to keep my feet the right way on the canvas, then move forward while ducking under the ropes. It's all about moving with my torso instead of just moving with my feet. Instead of backing up to avoid everything, I'm dodging it side to side, so that I can avoid a punch and still deliver a punch. Sounds easy at first, maybe. But I'm already frustrated because I'm having a hard time with it, especially as I move backward.

From that, we go to footwork, going around the gym. Kelley ties this thing that looks like a tube for a bike tire around my ankles so I can feel my feet easier and I can't cross them. It's a little weird, but I can see how he's trying to teach me how to keep my footwork and keep my leverage. This is way different from football. In football, I cross my feet all the time trying to get away from a bump by the cornerback. I'm so quick side to side with my feet that I can make guys miss so easy. Once I do that, I'm just running around them. But with this, I'm learning to use my body more to get free. It's going to be so cool to use this on corners.

In fact, what's so funny is that the first time I got in the ring to kind of spar with another guy, I froze. I completely froze, didn't know what to do. It just plays with your mind because you realize you're in this 16-by-16 space. It ain't like being on a football field, where you can go just about anywhere to get free. This is a tight-ass space, and you better know your shit or you're going to get knocked the fuck out. I can see that right now, so I'm not bullshitting my way through this stuff. Remember the time in warm-ups that I jumped, just for fun, on Orlando Brown from Baltimore? They call Orlando "Zeus" because the dude is huge. I mean like HUGE. He's like 6-foot-7, 360 pounds, big ol', nasty, ugly, tough-ass offensive lineman. The dude would probably still be playing in the league if that dumb-ass ref hadn't hit him in the eye with that flag. That was messed up. See, the flags are like beanbags, they have like little metal balls in them or something, just to make them a little heavy, and the ref threw a flag once at Brown and it hit Brown in the eye. Fucked up his eye really bad. That sucks.

Anyway, when I jumped on Brown, he didn't take that shit very well. He wasn't playing with me. All I hear is like, "What the hell are you doing?" I can tell right away, he's gonna kill me if he gets his hands on me, so I just get the hell away as fast as I can. Man, he might have pulled me apart like a roasted chicken if he got his hands on me. If I had been in a boxing ring with Zeus, that shit would have been scary.

And Kelley is awesome, 'cause he's like me. He loves to talk trash and he's into it. He's shouting "Ocho" every time I do something good, but he ain't afraid to tell me straight up that something ain't good enough. That's fine, that's what I'm paying him for. I'm telling you, I'm serious about this stuff. You know how they had the chicken in the *Rocky* movies and Sly Stallone was supposed to catch the chicken to improve his quickness? Kelley has this ball that's an odd shape and bounces funny. Same idea. You have to move quick to catch the ball off one of them funny hops. I'm getting it all and I'm sweating like crazy. By the end, I'm so tired I just drop to the canvas, exhausted. I've been moving for two hours straight, no more than a 30-second break to do all this stuff.

See, this is part of my ultimate plan. A couple of years ago, I raced a horse in Cincinnati at a track. Now, I did that for charity and had fun with that. I was dressed up in the jockey gear and all, red and black. I looked good as always. But that was just for fun. I beat the horse, but I was just goofing. But then I went on ESPN and I started talking trash about how I was going to move on to boxing and take on Floyd Mayweather Jr. The dude on ESPN was laughing, not taking me seriously. But I'm serious. I'm going to do this.

I'm going to perfect a lot of sports like this. It's like when I said I could beat Michael Phelps in swimming after the Olympics and people thought I was just talking shit. What I said is I knew three guys in Liberty City right now who could beat Michael Phelps. This is what I mean: There are guys all the time who are great athletes who don't have the discipline. They don't work at it and don't stay focused on it. But I have the discipline, so I would do it and I would beat Michael Phelps if I did the training. You know that commercial where the people wear those shirts, "I Am Michael Jordan," "I Am Tiger Woods"? I have one that says, "I Am Michael Phelps." Because I am Michael Phelps. What's so funny? I am. People won't see this until later. That's what I'm planning, a great television show where I take on other athletes at what they do. Track, basketball, Ping-Pong, whatever. But I'll play them and beat them at their sports because that's the type of athlete I am. I can't be stopped.

When we opened the season in Baltimore in 2008 after Phelps won the eight gold medals, I was going to have the "I Am Michael Phelps" T-shirt on. Then on the back it would say, "But I'm going for silver," and it would have had a picture of the Lombardi Trophy on it. He's from Baltimore, so I know the fans would have been all over that. They would have been yelling and cursing at me, but it would have been genius. Just would make me want to play that much harder. But Marvin heard about it and told me not to do it.

But I'm serious about a bunch of guys being able to beat Michael Phelps, and that's the sad part. We have so many people growing up with so much potential and they don't know how to get it out of themselves. We get guys stuck in the 'hood doing stupid shit all the time just to survive, and we could be doing so much more if we just could give them some help, show them how to focus, give them some skills. I know guys I grew up with who could easily be in the NFL playing right now. They would be serious players, but they didn't have the focus.

Man, it's the story about everything in the ghetto. Nobody has the skills to get out. It ain't about being smart. There's plenty of guys who are smart. Like I said, look at the drug dealers. Those guys know how to run a business. They know how to make money. Now, it's a rough way to go. You're probably going to get your ass shot if you don't get out at a young-enough age. That's just the way it is. But it's not like those guys don't have the desire to be successful, to make money, to help out their families, to do what they have to do. We could be taking those same dudes and turning them into real businessmen if we gave a shit. It's like Alonzo Mourning is always talking about, we spend all this money to put people in jail for doing shit, but we could spend that same money to make sure they get an education, do something else.

We could give some of those guys a better chance to make it in sports, too. Yeah, most of the guys in the 'hood, they either sell drugs or do sports, but a lot more would do sports if we had better programs. Shit, man, we got a bunch of brothers who don't even try to play baseball anymore. It's ridiculous. Anyway, here's my plan on all these other sports. I'm going to master them, one by one.

Just think about it. I had the passion for soccer that I have for football. No question. I could have been this good in soccer. But there's no money in it in the U.S., so what choice did I really have? I had to play football. That's why I had to focus on that. Now I'm ready to master something else. If I had tried to do two sports, it wouldn't have worked until now. I wouldn't have had time to be passionate about it. See, this is how I know Deion [Sanders] had to be special. To be able to play baseball and be good at it and be able to play football and be that great at it? Damn, that's what I'm talking about. He's gonna be a Hall of Famer in football, and he probably could have been a Hall of Famer in baseball if he really tried.

I'm starting with boxing, that's why I hired Kelley to train me. This ain't just to help me with football, even though it's going to do that. Kelley is working my ass so hard, cleaning up my footwork and my balance, all this shit that I've never had to worry about because my feet are so quick.

Anyway, it's the off-season and I'm 195. It's March and I'm at my playing weight. I'm working out twice a day. Kevin was a featherweight, a little dude who's quick as shit. I haven't been lifting with him, just going through two-a-days learning his stuff.

I like boxing. It's challenging my body, it's challenging me, especially at something that I have no clue about. Street fighting, yeah, I know that stuff. But I'm talking about organized, technique stuff. I'm a technician as an athlete. I love that side of it. On Day 3 I was already starting to really get it. Now I got frustrated and I was like, I want to just do it right now and keep on going until I get it right. I wanted to perfect it right then and there. But that's just me. It's like this tiny punching bag they have at South Florida Boxing. It's suspended by these tension lines that hold the bag, which is about the size of a volleyball, from the floor and ceiling. You hit it and it starts going back and forth real quick and you have to try to hit it clean.

The first day I tried to hit the bag, I couldn't hit it at all. I missed. I felt so unathletic. Then I was able to tap it, tap it, tap it, and finally hit it. In a week, I'll have it completely down. I guarantee you, I'm going to master this. I'm going to fight and I'm going to master it to a point that the swagger I have when it comes to football is going to transfer over to the ring. It's going to be so funny. I'm going to embarrass somebody at something I really don't do. Something you've been doing since you were 12. Racing the horse, that was just for fun. This is serious. I'm not going through these two-a-days for a month, paying Kevin Kelley however much I'm paying him, just to play. No, I'm not playing. And I'm not going to take a break. I'm going to Coach Collins in April, football for a month, then I'm going to see Floyd Mayweather Sr., Floyd's dad, and I'm going to do this, I'm going to keep it going until it's really time to go back to football.

Again, you don't think I'm serious, just listen. Listen to Kelley. The man knows his shit.

KEVIN KELLEY

two-time world featherweight boxing champion

Ocho has unbelievable feet. Unbelievable. He was so good that some of the boxers who were at the gym asked me, "Who's this dude with the great feet?" They didn't know he was Ochocinco. They didn't know he was a football player. We'd been at it for three days and they think he's a boxer already. Think about that, about how fast that is to pick up this sport. Me, I've been doing this since I was a teenager. I have studied this sport for almost 30 years, the ideas, the footwork, the leverage, the breathing techniques that help you recover. Chad has all the physical ability to be great at this. No joke. I ain't bullshitting. He learns so fast, picks up everything I'm talking about, sees it right away. And we're going fast, we're doing stuff in days that usually takes weeks.

But I think he loves how I do it. He loves it because I make it fun. I make it fast, keep it interesting. It's work in there, but you can't make it seem like work. You have to make it fun so that somebody wants to keep going. With Chad, you challenge his mind because he's smart, the physical part is the easiest part for him. He wants to know what the idea is that you're teaching, not just the move itself. But that's why he's so good at football, because you can see he cares about the details, how it works, not just how to do it and let's go. When he gets back to football, all of this work is going to make him so much faster it's going to be ridiculous. We'll take three or four seconds off what he does. Nobody will be able to catch him. Then we got to bring him out to Vegas to fight, get him to lose a little weight. He's a cruiserweight right now, but he doesn't need to go up to heavyweight. With his reach and quickness, we get him down to 178, he's fighting with Floyd and that'll be something. That will be fun.

I've been a champion twice. I got two rings. To get two rings, you don't just win the title, you have to win the title and then defend it five times. So it's like you have to win it five times over again. I've got 79 career fights. I've seen all the great fighters. I'm friends with all of them. Mike Tyson, Floyd Mayweather, Roy Jones, Prince Naseem Hamed. All of them. I'm telling you, Chad can fight. He has the ability to do this if he really wants to. It's all up to him. But you see him in the ring and you see the movement he has, how quick he picks things up. Yeah, it's different being in the ring and actually fighting, but he'll get that. Sky's the limit.

See, I told you. Now, I don't know what my contract says about boxing, but I don't care. You know why? Because whatever I lose on my contract, I'll make up for it on the gate for the boxing. No joke, I'll be huge in boxing. I'd be worth millions in just one fight. Serious, I could make $15, $20 million easy to fight somebody like Mayweather. Even better, I'll be like Naseem Hamed, the way he dances before a boxing match. Flamboyant? Naseem ain't got shit on me when it comes to flamboyant. I will put on a show that nobody will believe. It'll be Naseem meets Ray Lewis before the Super Bowl meets the best of *Dancing with the Stars.* I will destroy it, just kill it with the show I put on. People will buy my second fight just to see the dancing.

And this is just going to be the first step, my first real sport. When I get my reality show together, it's going to be awesome. I'm taking on everybody, boxing, basketball, track, Ping-Pong, whatever. The thing is, other athletes love this. They love the challenge. If you really think you're an *athlete,* you love this challenge, even if it's coming from somebody in another sport. I know it. You should have seen after the Olympics, this U.S. track chick Mary Wineberg challenged me in an interview. She runs the 400 meters and called me out to run the 400 against her. All I can say is, she better stay in shape.

The only thing I haven't really been able to get the hang of is golf. I tried it, but no, couldn't do it. Just not patient with it. Yeah, I know, big surprise about that. Tennis, I love. Soccer, that's my sport. Love soccer. Soccer is first. Basketball, I can hoop. With the right training, like I'm doing now in boxing, I can go play. I can play for real. I'm dead serious, I can play in the NBA, easy. I'm quick, quick as hell. Yeah, they're quick in the NBA, but I'm different quick. But, fuck yeah, I could play easy. It wouldn't take that long. I'm very athletic and I'm able to take what I do and transfer it into other sports, just like I do in boxing. It's like the dude who saw me in the gym and said I had unbelievable feet. Footwork is what most sports are about. That was a boxer who told me how quick I am, but my ability ain't coming from having been a boxer and training that way. It comes from doing it on the field. All that feet shit, that's all from Coach Collins. All of it.

It's not what he did, it's how he trained us. He trained me as a receiver to be like him. He's only like 5'10", and I'm like 6'2". I'm supposed to be a smooth route runner, I'm not supposed to have all these short, choppy steps. I run routes like the little dudes, using my feet to set up everything. Now I'm getting trained by somebody small and quick again. That means that as a boxer, they see me and I'm tall, but they don't expect me to be quick. But I'm learning from somebody small and quick. So with what I've learned and if I do box like I plan to, how am I going to do it? Small and quick like the guy who is training me. I'm one of the best in the NFL because of the stuff I learned from Coach C, and it's going to be the same thing with Kevin Kelley. I'm trying to match everything he's doing. Everything. He's 5-foot-8 and lightning quick, and I'm going to copy him and catch him. I am going to catch him, even though he's been doing it for 25 years. I'm going to catch him. I guarantee I will catch him. We have two more weeks to go.

It's like anything that involves that kind of coordination. Rollerskating? Oh yeah, I can roll. I can definitely roll. I like skating. The whole nine yards. Backward, forward, all the side-to-side stuff. I picked that up when I lived in Los Angeles. My mom skates. We used to go a lot. Now, on Sundays after games, I'll be all beat up from playing the game, but we go to the rink and we roll. That's my way of calming down after a game. I just roll and have a good time.

Just like I'm going to roll in all of these sports.

I find this sort of interesting about Chad. I've seen a lot of handwriting over the years, how players take notes and how coaches write notes to each other. Chad's penmanship is extraordinary, it's really elegant. He has the most elegant penmanship I've ever seen. Truly. Now, I don't know exactly what it means, but what I see in him is that he has the ability to really perfect certain things when he cares about it. He's the same way about football. He rarely makes mental errors, as long as he's careful to get the play. It's an attention thing. Certain things, he pays great attention to. When it came to school, you couldn't get him to care.

—**Bob Bratkowski,** Cincinnati Bengals offensive coordinator

FOURTEEN

WASTED DAYS AND WASTED NIGHTS

I TOLD YOU A little bit about how I grew up and how I dealt with school, which is to say that I only dealt with it as little as possible. About as little effort as I possibly could make. I drove my grandma crazy, since she was a teacher. After I got kicked out of Langston University and came home, she had enough. That's when she sent me out to California to be with my mom and work out school. She said to me: "You don't want to do it my way, OK, then you're going to have to go with your mother and figure out how to do it. You won't listen to me, you're not hearing what I have to say." She explained it again, like she has always explained it: "In order for you to get where you want to go, this is your last chance. Get your ass together, but you gotta do it. I can't take no more." She was fed up. She dealt with it ever since I was old enough to be in school.

That was harsh. I gotta say. She told me that stuff like a million times, and this was it. For her to send me to my mom, my grandma wasn't playing anymore. See, she knew what I wanted growin' up. She knew what I dreamed about doing. Lookin' back, I would have done it all over again and been completely different. To get an opportunity to play at a big school right away. Come on, that would have been awesome. For me to have gone to the University of Miami, Florida State, or Florida? I could have done this so much faster, probably been in the NFL a year or two earlier if I had just done it her way.

But this was a wake-up call for me. I noticed exactly what schools were saying. "We don't care who you think you are or what you can do." If I didn't do it their way, I wasn't going to play. That's it. That shit woke me up fast. It's just sad that it took that to happen to get my shit together.

Then again, I don't know if I would have gotten the training. I have the talent, no question. See, I was a late bloomer. My boys back in Miami will tell you that. It wasn't like I was dominating in Pop Warner. In high school, I didn't even play much until I was a junior or senior. My grandma took me to Miami Lakes to play Pop Warner. The guys in the neighborhood said I was playing out in the "suburbs." That's fine, let them have their fun. My brother Bo and friends like J. V. are always talking trash, especially when we're hanging out on South Beach or at the club, whatever. Bo was a quarterback in high school. He played at Jackson High. He was a year ahead of me. He'll tell you what I was like: "Yeah, Chad was pretty sorry when we were little. One time, our Pop Warner team was supposed to play his team and he didn't want to play us. He knew we were going to hit his ass all game. So he pretended he lost his cleats so he didn't have to play."

Or there's our buddy J. V.: "Man, Chad didn't even play his first two years in high school."

But that wasn't all bad, the way Bo explains it: "I think that's one of the reasons that Chad is so cool with everybody. You see it, guys will just walk up to him in the middle of the street in Miami. We ran into this dude on Washington Street, he had just arrived in Miami from out of town. He's a total tourist. He sees Chad and he freaks the fuck out. I mean, like, 'Oh my God, it's Chad Ochocinco. I've been in Miami for one day and I see Chad Ochocinco right here on the street! Ochocinco himself! Unreal.' For a lot of players, when they get that, they're like, 'Hey, good to meet you, later.' They don't want to be around that at all. Freaks them out a little. But Chad is so cool with those guys, and I think it's because people didn't kiss his ass when he was little, telling him how good he was. In fact, we all ragged on him like he wasn't shit, and I think because he didn't like that, he doesn't treat other people like that. He doesn't just blow people off like, 'Hey, you're not good enough to be around me.' He's not like that at all. I probably would be if I had made it because it was the other way for me."

Now, I get that. I am cool with most people I meet. I promised myself a long time ago that I would treat people OK, and I try to be that way. But what I didn't get, what I was hardheaded about, was school. The messed-up thing about me and school is I just always thought my way would work. I know colleges don't care that much about what your grades are. You'll find a place to play. It ain't like they want you to be a Rhodes scholar. They just want you to show up. My problem is, I didn't even want to show up. Like Coach Bratkowski said I told him, "I love football, I hate school." I did everything with school the hard way. Super backward.

It was unnecessary the way I did it, but I felt my way was going to work. I kept saying to my grandma, "Momma, I don't need school, I don't need school." I continued to fail and fail until I just tried it her way. But by this time, I'm at Santa Monica College, living in Los Angeles with my mother. My grandma is like, "Don't come back until you get your stuff together." Even then, I couldn't get eligible at Santa Monica. I was at Santa Monica for three years. Three years! At a junior college! See what I'm saying? I was wasting time. I played the '97 season, was ineligible in '98, and then finally got my shit together for the '99 season.

I finally said to myself, "Let me try it her way one time and see what happens." Of course, it's at the last minute where I'm at Santa Monica and it's do or die. Either I get it done now or I'm not going to be able to play Division I football. So I tried it her way for a semester, which is eight weeks, nine weeks long, and I did it real well. It worked. Damn, I should have been doing this shit from the start. I just couldn't dedicate myself to a long period of time to do something that I really had no interest in.

But the good thing about Santa Monica is that I got my shit together. Actually, Charles "Coach C" Collins got my shit together. He was my receivers coach at Santa Monica. He made me realize what my grandmother was saying. He made me get it. He taught me how to play, he got me up in the morning, he drove me to class.

CHARLES **COLLINS**

former assistant coach, Santa Monica College
and Cincinnati Bengals

I would liken it to getting a wild horse and trying to teach it to run in the Kentucky Derby. It's like you have to break it down and almost teach it how to run in the backyard before you can do anything with it. Chad is a good kid, didn't have problems like you see with a lot of guys, like drugs or alcohol. He was just untamed, wild, a guy with all this passion to play, but was all over the place. He needed mentorship. I was the person, the confidant he probably didn't have growing up in Miami. He didn't have much growing up. Yeah, he had his grandmother, but you know how that goes with kids, they don't listen to the grandparent until they really get in trouble. When I got him, it was probably the right time, because he had gone through a bunch of bullshit and ended up there. All he knew was that he wanted to play, but he didn't know how to get there, didn't know how to bottle that and get ready to really play.

As far as being a receiver, Chad had never really played receiver, he was coming at it completely new. He had been a quarterback in high school. With a guy who is like that, who is so passionate and so talented but so out there, you basically first have to put in some structure, teach him to be part of the crew, don't be the individual until you learn to play. You have to shake him up and say, this is how we do things. You have to show him how to prepare and practice. This is stuff that he should have learned in Pop Warner and in high school, but he didn't. He thought he knew how to do it from the start and that he knew better than I did. With a guy like that, you have to let him go fall on his face a few times and then they come back and say, "OK, Coach, what do you want me to do?"

When he came to me, he was a legend in his own mind, a guy with a big mouth who talks too much and nobody on the team likes. You'd look at him and say, "You have talent, but you have no clue about what you're doing." Finally, he gets to the point where he's ineligible to play, he comes to me crying, asking if I could help him and that's when he was ready. Basically, he didn't know what he didn't know and he had to find out. It's like with that wild horse, I had to break him first and teach him second. Take that talent and passion and teach him to channel, then give him some love. In a lot of ways, it was the same thing with Steve Smith, who's also a volatile guy. He's different than Chad, but they're both really emotional and tense. I had to beat them up at first, give them hard discipline, tough love, and then bring them back up.

The first thing was to get him to realize that he needed to get to class. Look, this was junior college. They're not trying to beat you down. If you show up and participate a tad, you can get out with a passing grade. But he was not getting his tail up in the morning to get to Santa Monica. He just wasn't there. He didn't have a work ethic and structure about just getting to school. I had to demand that of him. You're going to have to get the grades if you're going to play. Not everything is going to be handed to you. I had to get him up and get him to class. That was it. I had to do it. I had to call his house and then drive from my house in Pasadena to his place in L.A., 45 minutes, then drive 30 or 35 minutes to Santa Monica to get him there. I did that three times a week for two years. Over time, he has paid his debt to society for that. Chad has been pretty generous after what was done for him. He has done more than show his appreciation, coming to camps that I run. I do a camp for high school kids called the Phenom Factory, and he has helped with time and money to do that.

You have to understand his antics and what he's trying to say with the things he does. That's hard for some coaches who don't know his personality that well. It's like what he went through this last season with Cincinnati, when Marvin [Lewis] didn't let him play in the Pittsburgh game. He was late for a meeting, and Marvin felt like he had to do something to regain control of the team, that's what he said, so he told Chad he wasn't going to play. Well, you could kind of tell all week that Chad didn't really want to play, so either don't play him or find another way to reach him. Instead, Chad had Marvin completely frustrated to the point that Marvin didn't know how to react to him. Chad will do that to you. If Chad is having a bad practice, that hamstring is going to get tight. If it's a bad situation with a girl, something is going to happen. It's interesting how it comes out, but you have to figure it out. He's emotional, so he reacts first, then he thinks about what he's going to do. As a coach, if you don't figure it out, he's going to find that crack in what you're doing and he's going to push it as hard as he can. You have to pull it out of him sometimes and you have to be hard on him. If you don't, he'll run all over you.

That bravado, people misunderstand that stuff. He's just having fun. Sometimes it just goes over the top or he says something at the wrong time, when it's not appropriate, but the Bengals, they won't call him on it and jump on him about it. With me, I don't have to say "Hey" two or three times to get his attention. It's just once. But I have to do it right away. It's like him with those fucking gold teeth. Those gold teeth were part of his personality, they're his costume. When he had the gold teeth in, he would act out, do something stupid, and not concentrate. He put those in and all of a sudden he's Rasta Chad or Rapper Chad, whatever, his alter ego.

One time when we were getting ready for him to go in the draft, he came back down to work out with me. We're getting ready to practice, he's got all his little things and whatever, and he's got those fucking teeth in the bag. He walks away and I go over, grab the teeth, and just put them in my pocket. It's like, enough of this shit. He comes back and goes through the bag. I can see he's looking for the teeth, but I don't say anything. I'm just like, "What's going on? Let's go." He says, "I'm just looking for something, something's not in my bag." He won't tell me it's the teeth, because he doesn't want me to get on his case about it. So I say, "Whatever it is, cell phone or whatever, never mind, let's go." The first part of practice, it's like he can't function without the teeth, but eventually he picks it up. Later, as we're walking out, when he's not looking, the teeth go right in the trash.

The very next day, he comes back with another set of gold teeth. I'm thinking to myself, "Goddamn, he's just going to be some gold-teeth-buying motherfucker. I can't believe this shit." Years later, I told him I did that and he's like, "Coach C, you threw my teeth in the trash? Man, come on." But that's how you have to handle Chad. You have to cut off an area. Some of his stuff, you can let it go. The celebrations and some of the personality stuff, as a coach, you might not like it, but that's him. But you don't compromise on the effort, the fundamentals, the technique. Those are things that are going to save him late in games when teams are trying to take him out of his game, take things away from the offense. As long as he's playing hard and doing those things, I just let him be who he is. But you better have those hips sunk when you're running your route, you better not compromise on the effort, you better cross the safety's fuckin' face when we run a skinny post. You have to corral those antics in his route running. When you run that double move, you better plant your fuckin' foot in the ground. I started like that with him a long time ago, and I think the guys in Cincinnati were pretty surprised when I talked to him like that when I first got there and he didn't talk back. I can honestly say, he has never said "Fuck you" to me, because he knows I started with him way back when, kicking his ass about that. He may talk a little, and I'll listen, but there's only so far he's going to go. I give him a look like, "Motherfucker, don't even think about it," and he knows, if it has to be checked or corrected, he better do it. That's because of the relationship we have, the connection we developed a long time ago and that took a lot of time.

That's why I am who I am. That's what I was dealing with at Santa Monica. Coach C and Head Coach Robert Traylor. Those men took care of me. Coach Traylor would be on my ass all the time, too. I'd hang around the football office all the time and he'd be like, "Do you ever go to class?" It's like Coach Traylor said: "Chad needed a lot of attention when he was with us. We had him and Steve Smith, and they both gave us a run for it in different ways. Steve was more intense, going to school actually did mean something to him, and he took care of his business a lot easier than Chad did. Chad wanted to be the class clown. He needed to be noticed."

And Santa Monica was good for me in other ways, because I really did have to learn to deal with other people, talented people. Steve Smith is a great example. I talk to Steve a lot now. We're friends, but we're real different. Steve is intense, super intense, and we got in a fair share of scrapes at Santa Monica. I didn't understand what he was about back then and he didn't understand what I was about, clowning all the time and joking. But Steve is a guy who is so physical and wants to win so bad. He's going to clock somebody's ass from the other team. Steve is my dude and he is difficult. Steve is a hard-ass. He's always so serious. I'm like, "Take a chill pill, Steve."

And in football, he loved to hit, very physical for a guy who is so small [Smith is 5-foot-9, 185 pounds]. He was like that when we were in college, just like he is now, how violent he is running the ball. He's looking for contact. He has always been that way. Always. He hurt his neck at Utah hitting somebody, but he's still the same way. Probably after the injury he got that much stronger in that area. He's a beast, dude. His style of play, I couldn't do. The same with T. J. I couldn't play that way, the way they do. My style of game is completely different. If I did that, I'd be in the hospital. But the thing I learned with Steve was how to be part of a group. We had a great group of receivers, five dudes who could all play, and we learned to help each other.

Most important, we drove each other. We all thought we were the best, and we fed off that shit.

STEVE **SMITH**

Carolina Panthers Pro Bowl wide receiver

Chad has never changed from what I knew of him in junior college. He always believed that he was the best, and the good thing about that is that I understood his deal and why he was the way he was. He's also a Florida guy who was trying to fit in in L.A. New place, new set of friends, new people. Originally, me and Chad bumped heads a lot. Not fistfights, but arguments. He thought he was the best and I thought I was the best. The good thing is that I look back on it and realize we pushed each other. He wanted to be the best, so he worked hard. I wanted to be the best, so I worked hard. So it worked for both of us.

I know I needed to get out of there, get myself in a place where I wasn't around, just hanging out in a place where I could do stupid stuff. And Chad had the same mind-set as well. We had our dislikes about each other's personalities at the time, but on the football field it was five of us [among the wide receivers] and we were a hard bunch to deal with as far as cornerbacks covering us. We used to run the wrong routes all the time, and our best plays came off us running the wrong plays as a group. As a group, we would talk down to any [defensive back] crew. We didn't care. We would run plays where if Chad or Eugene Sykes had a crossing route and I was supposed to clear out [run a deep pattern], I would never clear out. Chad would bring his guy across and I would wait and just clean his guy up. Just try to kill his guy, and that left Chad with only my guy to beat. We ran that play all the time. It was ridiculous. I'd go about 10 yards, wait, wait, wait, peel back, and just blow his guy up, just unload on him, pow. If a guy on the other team pissed us off, we'd run that play and just clean him up. The linebacker, the corner, whoever. It was more my play. Chad didn't do that. That was my deal. I liked doing that. We used to love it. We got somebody on every team. We'd run it once a game and then those guys would be looking for us the whole time.

But Chad was a trip, man, a real trip. He had his suits, his Florida suits. There was one game he didn't play. He hurt his shoulder and couldn't play. So he wore this lime-green walking suit. It was that Florida green, kind of washed out, like you see all them colors on South Beach. That didn't fly at all. It was horrible. Horrible. It was the worst outfit I have ever seen him wear. Terrible. But Chad is a good dude. I can hear him in my head and I just start laughing. Yeah, he has that alter ego and sometimes he'll go there. One thing I love about Chad is, because I know him on a different level, he hasn't really changed. He's the same guy. Some people say that's a problem. To me, no, Chad is all right. I always know I'm dealing with Chad. He's the same. He's good. The only thing he does to mess with me is that he'll call me and say, "It's eighty-five." Or he'll say, "It's Ocho." Or maybe, "It's Ochocinco." I say, "Who?" He'll say, "It's Chad." I refuse to talk to his alter ego. I won't do that. He's Chad. I won't talk to him until he's Chad. I talk to Chad.

Damn, Steve will talk to whoever the hell calls his phone. Whoever I want to be, he's going to talk to me. But Steve is right about how we pushed each other. Now, you think about that crew, but we were nowhere near what we would be based on what we are now in the NFL. Not even close. I'm telling you. We could catch it and we can run, and that's it. That's basically what everybody could do at that point. Man, that's like right out of high school, so we were nowhere near what you would think. But when you say Steve Smith and Chad Ochocinco on the same team, you think of what you are seeing now and try to picture it back then. We weren't even the best receivers on our team. A friend of mine, rest in peace, Demetrius Posey, was the best. He was from Venice High, out that way. A big dude, kind of like Terrell Owens is now. He died in a car crash.

Anyway, that was my experience at Santa Monica. That shit was important to me and my development. I had people go way out on a limb to help me. But I still had to get my ass to a Division I college. I barely made it through, but Coach C had a coach he knew up at Oregon State, so he got me on up there. I had one other option, that was to go to Hawaii, but that shit wasn't going to happen. No way. I was already 3,000 miles from Miami, I wasn't getting on a plane to fly another five hours to play ball. Could you imagine, every road game is a five-hour flight? Hell no.

I had some classes and shit to finish up my last semester at Santa Monica, so I didn't show at Oregon State until like August, and I've got one season of eligibility left. That's it. That's all I have to prove to the NFL I can play. This is total make-or-break. What helps me is we have one good fucking team. We had me and we had T. J., who went on to be my teammate at Cincinnati. Like me, T. J. is a junior college transfer, so we're both starting off from behind the eight ball. Neither one of us has time to fuck around. The other good thing is we have coach Dennis Erickson running the show at Oregon State. Denny E. is cool, totally cool. He loved junior college guys.

So we got me, T. J., and DeLawrence Grant, who played with Oakland. We had Nick Barnett, who's starting with Green Bay, as a freshman playing on special teams. We were nasty. They had never seen shit like this in Corvallis. We were unreal, changing school history. Then again, I had never seen anything like Corvallis, at least not for that long. Yeah, I was at Langston in the middle-of-nowhere Oklahoma, but that was for like a month. I was in Corvallis for four months. I had never done shit like that.

And I never did shit like I started to do about four games into the season. Like I said, I had four months to make an impression on the NFL, to prove that I could play. After about four games, we were playing in Washington and I made two huge plays and now I'm starting to roll. More important, we're rolling. We go 11–1 that season and finish No. 4 in the country. No. 4? Oregon State? I'm serious, Oregon State holds records for like the longest losing streak in Pac-10 history, and we go 11–1. I catch 37 passes for 806 yards and eight touchdowns. We go to the Fiesta Bowl to finish the season against Notre Dame and we just smoke them. I caught a 74-yard touchdown pass in that game. Coach Erickson got on my case because he thinks I spiked the ball before I got in the end zone. Whatever, no replay, it's good. Playing for Denny E. was good.

DENNIS ERICKSON

former Oregon State and current Arizona State head coach

Chad was good for us, that's obvious. He was very confident, a lot of God-given talent, and he came in knowing he had to impress. He was there for one semester to prove himself, and he knew it. He worked hard. Yeah, he was a character. He pulled the gold teeth out every once in a while and became that guy from where he was from, the guy who grew up in Miami. He'd liven things up like that. He did it mainly in practice, never in a game. . . . The one thing about Chad, he knew where he wanted to go. He knew his success in life was about being a professional football player. Now, he was only there a short time and people can say what they want to about whether that was a good thing or not, but as soon as he got drafted and he signed, he gave $50,000 to our football program to help us keep going. I don't know too many people who do that right away. He appreciated what he got there, even if it was only for a short time.

By the end of the season, I got invited to the Senior Bowl, which is where I met Coach Bratkowski when he was still coaching for Pittsburgh. That's when I told him that I don't do drugs, I don't smoke, I don't get in trouble, I love football, and I hate school. We still talk about that from time to time. The NFL had all these questions about me. It was 2001 and I'd never been anywhere for very long. I had no track record. Then some draft people start to pay attention to me. I made Mel Kiper's all-sleeper list. I'm thinking, "Sleeper? I'm not a sleeper." I didn't get that. I thought I did enough to be a first-round pick. I even did an interview with Kiper back then and I said what I say now: "If football wasn't a part of my life, there were three things that could have happened, and they were all bad. I would have likely been selling drugs, in jail, or dead. I know I caused my grandmother to have a lot of sleepless nights worrying about me and the direction I was headed."

After the Senior Bowl and all the workouts, the NFL combine and everything, I went back to Miami for the draft. We were having a party at my grandma's house, waiting for me to get drafted in the first round. So we're waiting and waiting and waiting. David Terrell from Michigan goes No. 8 to Chicago. Koren Robinson at No. 9 to Seattle. Rod Gardner at No. 15 to Washington, and then the Jets trade up to No. 16 to get Santana Moss from the University of Miami. They get in the twenties and finally Freddie Mitchell from UCLA goes No. 25 to Philadelphia. Freddie Mitchell? Then Reggie Wayne from Miami goes to Indianapolis at No. 30 before the first round ends.

I don't get picked. That's when I went to a little room toward the back of my grandma's house and realized all the shit that I had screwed up, how I messed up my chance to be a first-round pick. Fortunately, I didn't have to wait much longer. One more receiver [Quincy Morgan] went before me, but the Bengals took me with the fifth pick in the second round, No. 36 overall. I was a Bengal, and I couldn't be happier than I was then. Yeah, it burns me that seven wide receivers got drafted before me. What, maybe two of those guys are even in the league anymore, that's Santana Moss and Reggie Wayne. But think about what else—I could have been one of those two guys if I had just listened way back when in high school. I could have been Moss or Wayne if I had just listened to my grandma and done the school thing in high school instead of wasting like eight years. Shit, I might have been drafted in 1999 if I had my shit together and really listened. That's the lesson in all of this.

Anyway, I sign with the Bengals and it's all good. I'm getting ready to play in the NFL. When I do finally arrive, it's amazing. The moment I walked out of that tunnel that first time I was in the NFL and saw those 70,000 people, I said, "This is me, this is mine, this is what I was meant to do." Some people get scared that first time. Me? Scared, my ass. I was loving it. I walked out the first time, butterflies, looked around like I was lost. I just thought, "How can I find a way to make every person in here embrace what I'm all about?" And I've done that. I might have pissed a couple people off along the way, but you know, one touchdown and they'll always be back. Everything will be cool. The first time Chad walks out there and catches a pass and goes to the house, everybody's going to be fine.

What people don't understand is that I have to be this way. I have to be on the edge all the time. I love that. I love putting myself out there for people to look at, to cheer for, to boo. They can hate me if they want to, but really everybody loves me. They love what I'm about because I'm about fun. I'm like that guy up on the tightrope. I'd be that guy up there, do it with no net. Why? Because I can't fail. I will not fail. I'm too afraid to fail to let that happen.

That's the way it has to be if you want to be great. You can't be great by not taking chances. You have to dazzle people. You have to push it and push it and push it. All the time. Like I said, I love me some me. Even if I got here the hard way.

I love the whole attitude. It's kind of rocky sometimes when you're a fan of Chad, like when he talks about how he wants to get traded. But you have to be on board with the whole program. You can't like Chad just a little. You have to love the whole person.

—**Stacey Davis,** Bengals fan from Dayton, Ohio

FIFTEEN

FAMILY AND FRIENDS

AS I SAID BEFORE, there aren't a lot of people out there who I trust. I have my brother Bo, my brother Chauncey, my grandmother, my brother Sam Brown, and maybe two others. There's Maya, too, but that's different even from those guys. These are guys I grew up with, who I hang out with, guys I have around me at the clubs in South Florida or when we go out in Cincinnati. I bring about 30 guys to Cincinnati twice a year. They come for a big weekend, Friday to Monday, take care of them all, have a good time. I've done it every year since I've been with the Bengals. Just a little tradition.

Even those guys, I don't trust them all. Don't get me wrong, they're good dudes, friends of mine and such. I like them, but it's just a little different. They're not all in that real tight group, that inner circle I have. Bo is. Bo is important to me. He's a year older than me and we have the same dad, but not the same mom. We hang out a lot and he watches out for me. Like we'll be at a club and I'll be trying to make everybody happy, get everybody drinks. I'll buy like eight bottles of wine and six bottles of Grey Goose, a bunch of bottles of something else. It's a party. Now, I'm not drinking. Maybe have cranberry juice. Sometimes a Red Bull to get going. But I don't know how much we need of whatever. But then Bo will be back there, giving me that look like, "Cut it, that's it, you've done your share." Bo is good that way, looking out for me and checking up on me, making sure that people don't take advantage.

Plus, Bo gets it. When I was struggling, he used to send me money. That was way back when he was doing what he had to do to make money and helping me out. He took care of me. Now it's switched and I'm able to help him. But the thing is that Bo takes care of business. He's making money on his own, supporting himself. I respect that. Chauncey, hey, he's chillin', or as Bo puts it, "Chauncey is loose." Chauncey is a free spirit all the way, all the time.

I'll let Bo tell it a little more. But let me say this, Bo is a beast. Full-on beast. He's built, massive shoulders, big and strong. He's in great shape, and that's why he's training athletes now down in South Florida.

BO JOHNSON
Chad's brother

Chad has always really gotten it. He understood what he wanted and how to get there. He just knew. It's like during his second year in the league. I was at the hotel, standing out on the balcony and smoking a joint. Hey, that's the truth. I'm not hiding that. It was a long time ago and that's what it was. But Chad came out there and looked at me and said, "Bo, they want to pay us to do what we've always loved to do. They want to pay us to play. Why don't you just put that down, get into shape, and try to make it?" I never really looked at it that way. Chad gets the picture of what he wants in his life and he goes after it. He may not have been great in school, but he's smart and he knows how to discipline himself when he really wants something.

That's his story in football. He's focused, really focused. During the season, he doesn't mess around. It's all football. That's all he thinks about. That's all he does. Every week he's like that. He'll tell everybody back home, "Hey, once the season starts, I don't want to hear any bad news. I don't want to know about that stuff. If somebody died or they're in jail, tell me after the season." Serious. We'll go out to a club on Friday night in Cincinnati and he's just sitting, thinking about the game, how he's going to play, what he's going to do. There's people all around, good-looking women, everything, and he's just in another world. When we go to the mall, he'll be like walking around the mall, pretending that the people in there are defensive players, and he'll be making moves on them like it were the game. Some of it is really funny. He's a trip to watch when he's doing that. The first couple of times he did it, I'm like, "What the hell are you doing?"

We'll all go to dinner that night at J. Alexander's, his favorite restaurant. Then we'll go to the Ritz, a club. Saturday night, we're at the hotel and he'll come in to see all the guys and thank everybody for coming down for the game. Like he has to thank us when he's paying the whole way. But that's how he does it. That night, all of us, except Chad, will go to The Mix, another club. The game is Sunday and then, after the game, we go to Annie's, this big warehouse that they turned into a bar. After that, we'll all go skating to unwind.

But this is just the way that Chad stays connected to everybody. This is what he does to take care of the crew, make sure he remembers everybody from back home. Like I said, we got an interesting group. When we're all out, it's a story every night. Every damn night is something funny. One night, he had this cop call his girlfriend, Maya, and say, "Chad has been arrested and he'd like you to come bail him out." It sounded all official. But she knows he's just being stupid and she says, "Well, does he have his [engagement] ring on. Yes? Well, that's fine, you can just let him sit there." She got him right back.

With our dad, all they can ever really talk about is football. There's nothing else for them to communicate about and there's not much communication. It's like Chad said, he doesn't have a relationship with our dad. That's just the way it is for a lot of guys in the 'hood. What are you going to do about it? You going to whine and cry about it? It just is what it is. Whining and crying ain't going to help. Look, Papa was a rolling stone and that's it. It's like most of the time, I don't know where he is. It's not like our dad is keeping in touch. One of us will hear from him, but it's not like he was ever around for any of us that long. He just did his thing. For kids who grow up in the 'hood, our coaches were our fathers. Those are the guys we looked up to for that kind of guidance, on how to act like a man.

But Chad's grandma, Paula's mother, she was the one who provided the place that was safe for everybody. Grandma didn't mess around and her house was the safe place in the neighborhood, the stable house. She didn't put up with no bullshit in that house. Man, she'd run us out of there if we didn't do what she wanted. She had a video game in the house, it had all the old games on it, like Asteroids, Centipede, Pac-Man, all that stuff. Her house was the place people hung out.

Bo is right about the father-figure stuff, and that's been a big issue for me as I've gotten older and my kids are growing up. I'm figuring out how to be a dad as I go along. I've got four kids with three different women. My oldest is my daughter Gigi, who's 11. Then there's C. J., who's 11 and is my son. He lives in Los Angeles with his mother. Then there's my girls, Chadé, six, and Chaiel, four. Gigi's mom is Tricc, who I met in high school, back when I was a real asshole and didn't know shit. C. J.'s mom is LaRhonda, and I had the last two girls with Kenyada.

It's not the way you want it to be, but you learn things as you're growing up. You think it's OK because that's how you were raised, and then you get older and you realize, I can't keep doing this. That's enough kids to take care of and enough people to be involved with.

I don't spend the time I should or really take out enough time to spend with them, but when I do we have a blast. I pick them up from school when I can. I don't know. The moms fuss at me all the time about spending more time with them. All the time. Some days they tell me, "I need a break." With all the time I spend away from them, I should be a lot better at it, but I haven't got there yet. I haven't grasped the concept of what being a father is. I'm very good with the financial part. But then they want the other part of it, which money can't really do. The moms want that. The funny thing I always tell them is that if it was the other way around, if I didn't have anything to offer but I was there all the time, had time to be with them, they'd be fussing about me not having the money. It goes either way, there's always something to fuss about. I told them I'll get better at it. I will.

And I really haven't taken the time out to thank the moms, because they could do some damage. If they wanted to, they could try to take all my shit, but I've been good to them, I've done right by my kids, and I think that might be one of the reasons why the moms have never really done that. I don't think that was their intention in dealing with me anyway, because they were here before the storm. I would call this a storm. They were here with me when it was calm and I was just Chad "Who the fuck is Chad? Who is he?" Ochocinco. I think that might be part of the reason also.

My kids are my motivation out on the field on Sundays. The mothers complain a lot about the time that I'm not there, but I think the things that I sacrifice now are going to make life better for them later. That's how I feel. The legacy I create and the things that I do here are going to make it that much easier for them later on. That's the way I see it. I see it different from them, and I know I missed out on a lot of time that won't be able to be made up, but it's like I'm here, and I'm trying to do something different than what I had. Whatever it is I'm doing, I know it's going to work. The mothers say that's good and they respect that and whatever, but I have to find a way to spend time. That's the only complaint I get. I do spend time, but not enough. Nowhere near enough. I see them every week, as much as I can.

My kids are hilarious. I don't spend the time I should, but when I do, it's some of the funniest stuff. They are funny. My kids can do whatever they want. When they are with me, go ahead. They're not going to do much when they are with me anyway, but I let the mothers be the discipline. When they grow up, I want them to know I'm not the one that beat you. I'm the good guy. It's Planet Chad, everything is fun. That's all it's about. The thing that's so funny is I never scream at my kids, but when their moms are calling me and telling me, "So-and-so is doing this," as soon as I say something in any kind of tone that's not normal, what do you think any of my kids start doing? Crying, right away. Right away. As soon as I say something, "Man, what are you doing?" And they let it all out, because I never discipline them. To me, that's the advantage of picking and choosing your battles with your kids.

My youngest daughter, Chaiel, is just like me, built like me, big calves, strong. She's the athlete, always running and jumping on things. Chaiel is a character. She talks trash just like I do. She will tell me stuff, man. She's ahead of her time a little bit with the comments on stuff she hears and she sees. She talks at me, but I get it together quick. Chadé is more laid-back, relaxed, the girly type who wants to get her nails and feet done. Gigi is cool, she's just laid-back. Likes to dance and is always doing pageant. It's a gospel, modern-dance thing and she can really dance. Typical young-girl stuff. She's a good girl. C. J. is playing football and running track. I told his mom to keep him as busy as you can, put him in everything you can. I'm going to be down there all of April and watch him run track. Football goes on the same time I play, so I can't see him. I'm never able to catch that, but I will at some point.

Tricc was my girlfriend from high school. She had Gigi when I was in college, so I was gone. That's the time I was fuckin' up. There was no way I was coming back. That was the bad years, when I was an asshole, when Grandma sent me away. C. J. was born in L.A. and I wasn't around. I was on a plane when Chaiel was born. Chadé was the only one I was there for. We went to the hospital at like six in the morning. It was cool. Seeing the birth was nasty. They hand her over to me and I'm like, what am I supposed to do with this now? But then it was a great feeling. That was something. I'm holding a little me. Just having little me's around is cool. No lie, I think that's very cool. I love that. I also think that kids have slowed me down a little. Not that I was out of control in any way. I wasn't out of control other than having kids in that way. I just like the thought of the little ones and watching them grow.

When I had my first child, I was 19. I wasn't scared. Scared for what? I had my grandma behind me, so there was nothing to be scared of. Whether I had a child or not, I had to get on the right path to my career and I was still figuring it out. Like I said, I was fucking up left and right in school, but I knew what I wanted to do and how I had to do it. I also knew I had to throw myself into that to make it work. I've been lucky because the individuals I'm dealing with, the moms, are pretty cool with me. Of course, they want more. Bo said he thinks they're hanging around, hoping that I will choose to be with them all the time, that things will get bad when they realize that's not going to happen. I don't know, I think I've been pretty straight with them about what I want to be and what I'm doing. For me, I'm out of the kid business now. You have to grow out of that and realize, this is enough. I've talked to Ray Lewis about it. He's pretty much the same as me, has his kids, takes care of them, provides for them, but he drew a line once he got to a certain age.

For me, I have to be careful how many people I'm letting into my life. It's not just about women, it's all people. Look, I'll be cool with all these people who come around me. It's not like I'm A-Rod or Tiger Woods walking into some places, where people just go crazy and rush at me. I'm not being chased down by the paparazzi. Come on, this is Cincinnati. People will walk up and it's like, "Man, I really respect your game, and I like what you do." Everybody likes the trash talking and being able to go out there and back it up. It's not crazy. I'll treat them OK and be nice. But I'm not going to trust you. I don't trust many people around me. You can't get close, you just can't. That's who I am. If you weren't here before I made it, there's no reason to try to get close now. The people I trust are the people who were around me before I had anything, who liked me for just me. You could say that makes my world a little smaller, but I don't see it that way. I just watch the people who I allow to get close. It takes a whole lot for me to let somebody in. Like what it took with Maya and her situation. That was unique. I know a lot of people, I hang with all sorts of people. That doesn't mean that they have to get close to me.

Out of all those guys who are trash talkers, I like him the best. I can accept what he does. He's talking trash in a way that's fun and makes it entertaining, I think. He might put his foot in his mouth once in a while, but who doesn't? He does it in a way that he's not trying to hurt anybody like some other guys, but we won't name names. He's not ripping his coaches or his quarterback. Chad is a competitor and he's always open, but that's every great player. Every great receiver is always open.

—**Tony Gonzalez,** Kansas City Chiefs Pro Bowl tight end

SIXTEEN

PLANET CHAD

TONY G. IS RIGHT on the mark. I am always open. I have never once been covered in my entire career. No lie. Now, you think that's absurd. You think I'm stupid crazy. Whatever, you don't get it. You don't understand the world I live in. You don't understand the confidence I have. You don't understand my ability.

You don't live on Planet Chad.

Now, how awesome would that be? Planet Chad would be the place. It would be like nothing you've ever seen. The City of Gold? Shit, the world of gold. Off the chain times 10 million. There would be no rules. How the fuck do I say it? No limits. In a good way, no boundaries. You push the envelope at whatever you're doing. That would be a very, very flamboyant planet. Flashy. My planet would be made of gold. It would.

Street made of gold, lightposts made of gold. That would be sweet. Speed limit? For what? Ain't no speed limit for me now. My streets would be called like Usain Bolt Way. I like that one. Red lights? No. Stop signs? No. You're on your own. You know, like the cartoons where they have all the cars speeding and speeding and they never get in an accident? That would be my planet. No traffic tickets on Planet Chad. Hell, no police. What do you need police for? Nobody is going to hurt anybody. Not on Planet Chad. Planet Chad is about having fun. Naked women. Hugh Hefner's All-Playmates Squad. Man, we probably don't even need strip joints, even though I love strip joints. Tootsie's, Pure Platinum, the Rollexx, Cheetah, Solid Gold . . . you name 'em, I love 'em.

Who works on Planet Chad? That's a good damn question. That's why I couldn't have a planet. My planet would be unorganized as hell. It would. It would be all over the place. But it would be the place where everybody from every other planet would want to visit. It would be the vacation planet where everybody would want to be. You could see it:

"You ever been to Planet Chad?"

"No."

"Dude, you gotta check that shit out, it's unbelievable."

You can do whatever you want. Beaches, mountains, parks, whatever you need. No drugs on Planet Chad. You do drugs, you're kicked off the planet. A lot of cigars. A lot of Frank Sinatra. All kinds of music. I don't drink, but there would be alcohol.

Houses are monstrosities, 35,000 square feet, big aquariums, huge lakes around every house. In fact, Planet Chad is on water. Or surrounded by water. A whole planet surrounded by water. And everything is shaped like an 85. The coral in the sea. The trees. It's Atlantis, but 100 times better. I really should try to build that.

Football on Planet Chad? It would be a big play on every play. Go deep, throw slants that go to the house. Every play, big. No replay. No stopping the game. Replay sucks because everything stops. The game clock would be 85 minutes. Make it 8.5 seconds per play, it would be playing constantly. No standing around in the huddle. Get to the line and go. All-out blitzes by the defense, man coverage all the time. Could you imagine me as the commissioner of the National Football League? Oh damn, that's unreal. Now, the real deal is that I'm already like the king. Actually, I'm the king, sultan, rabbi, priest, the almighty everything. Whatever you want to call me. There'll be like 16 words in my title, like the Flintstones with the Grand Imperial Poobah. But as the Grand Imperial Ochocinco, I run the NFL.

The rules against celebrations, gone. In fact, if you don't celebrate or talk shit, you get fined. Well, maybe not. It's like that rule I talked about with having a celebration competition. You only get to celebrate if you win that *Dancing with the Stars*–type competition. But if you're one of those guys, you better go off. You better do some unreal shit every week. You better be original, you better make it look good, you better get the fans off their butts and whooping it up. If you're on the road, you better piss off the home fans, get their asses riled up. We want pandemonium in the stands. It's got to be crazy-ass loud.

Oh man, could you imagine how hard everybody would play on Planet Chad? Every game would be like the intensity of the Super Bowl. The hype, the trash talk. My checklist of cornerbacks I did a couple of years ago? That would be old-school on Planet Chad. That's like stuff they would do in high school or Pop Warner. Pregame would be crazy. People would come to the games like three hours early just to get seats for pregame. And the best thing is, they'd all go home happy. Even if your team lost on Planet Chad, you had a good time. Sure, it sucks to lose, but you're still talking about that big play at the end or that great celebration by your boy Ochocinco in the second quarter, when I danced on the crossbar of the goalpost and then did a double somersault to the ground and stuck the landing. Oh man, it would be intense.

And all contracts would be negotiable at the end of every season. Hey, man, that's the way it is. It's like with me, I can outplay that long-term deal. I'm going to continue to outplay that deal. When I outplay it, I get to come back to the table. Hey, teams get to do that if they think you're not playing up to what you're supposed to do. You have a certain receiver that, if he stays healthy—which he has, which he will—it shouldn't matter if he has a long-term deal. When I outplay it year after year, I can come back to you and redo it. Yeah, people say I should just sign a one-year deal, but it doesn't work like that. You give me what you give me, I'm going to show you. I'm going to outplay what you are giving me and show you how underpaid I am, and I expect you to redo it. The way the NFL is set up, the owner doesn't have to renegotiate. But on Planet Chad, they do. Just think how much I'd be worth on Planet Chad. Some people would say I'm full of it, but we have so many that are willing to give me what I deserve. We saw that last off-season. You had Washington, Dallas, and Philadelphia. Washington was willing to give up two first-rounders and the Bengals didn't take it. That's unheard of, that a team would say no to that.

Basketball would be dunks and alley-oops all the time. We'd have like a four-point line, too, like from 30 feet, really push the limits. Take the "And 1" players and put them in the NBA. That would be exciting. Yeah, defense might be a problem for my guys in the NBA, but defense is bullshit anyway. It's all gotta be man defense. No double teams, none of that sorta zone shit that they play right now.

Now, some people think this is just stupid, and, yeah, some of my ideas are just funny, except for the no-speeding-tickets thing. That's for real. But the funny part about the sports thing is that it's kind of like that in other places. Look at soccer around the world. That's the biggest sport in the world. You'd think it would be all sacred, like how some people treat football in this country. But the great thing about soccer is that people take it seriously, but they have fun. I mean FUN. The singing by the fans. You got like 200,000 people singing one song all at the same time. It's awesome over there. The gambling, they don't pretend. You can gamble on the games right there at the stadium. It's not like the NFL, where we pretend that we don't know that people are out there gambling. Shit, it's like fantasy football. You hear some fans over here say, "Oh, fantasy football is bad. It's not what the game is about." That's BS. It's another way for people to get into the game, to get excited about it.

And, like I'm telling you, the celebrations in soccer make the stuff I do look like kindergarten. Man, they just live for it and enjoy. Soccer is pure joy over there. Really, if you asked me my dream life, I would have been a soccer player. Soccer is my first love. I've got friends in soccer, too. Thierry Henry, Ronaldinho, Christiano Ronaldo, lots of those guys. I got to hang out for a couple of weeks with Henry in England and that was sweet. Just the way that the Europeans look at soccer is totally insane, over the top. I think God comes second over there. First is soccer, then comes God. It's sweet. You go to a match and it's like 200,000 people and they stand up the whole time and sing the team songs the whole game. If I could be out there playing for Arsenal or in Barcelona, man, that would be sweet.

The way that they look at soccer players in Europe versus how we look at football players here is totally different. The treatment that David Beckham gets over here, he gets 100 times more attention over there. You might as well just have rose petals laid at their feet when they walk around in Europe. It's just total love and adoration for the soccer players, but it's not like they can't go anywhere. Like Henry, he could just hang out, go to a club, and it would be cool. He didn't need like an entourage or anything. Those guys can really show their personality without worrying what people are going to think.

And the thing is, the soccer fans know the game so well. They understand it and they know how to criticize. They'll boo and talk shit and let players know it. They don't screw around. If their team isn't trying to win, if management isn't doing everything, they get it and they don't blame the players. It's not like in this game, where all of a sudden a team can be bad for years and it's clear that management doesn't get it and then people start blaming the players. I mean, come on, let's get serious. It's like with me. We've been getting worse over the past three years and people are looking at me like I'm the problem because I speak my mind about what's going on. I get upset and it's like, "Oh, he's a distraction, he's the reason the team is falling apart." Look, it's easy to blame the flashy, extravagant, trash-talking black guy and forget that a lot of other stuff goes into running a team. Or maybe remember that the team went 8–8 four straight years with me around and we made the playoffs once.

That may not sound like a big deal and it's really not like some big-ass accomplishment, but think about this: The last time that the Bengals had four straight seasons going .500 or better was from 1972 to 1977. I wasn't even BORN YET! For the 10 years before I got here—a whole decade—they didn't have one winning season and they were .500 once. In the last 18 years, we've made the playoffs once.

And I'm the problem? Give me a fucking break. Do you understand why I want out a little better? Do you understand why I dream about something else rather than just being happy with all the stuff I have? Do you understand what I'm out here for? Yeah, I play for money, but I want to win. I want to win so bad because I know what comes with it. I dream about that.

Yeah, the coaches can talk all they want about how I wasn't recognizing coverages or not playing well or whatever. But Coach C [Charles Collins] gets it. He knows. He'll tell you: "This last season [in 2008], Chad wasn't on top of his game. He wasn't paying attention to the coverages, how they were rotating or how the other team might be setting up a fire-zone blitz, and I'm going to tell him that. But honestly, the Bengals needed to trade him. They need to let him go. Yeah, they're killing his spirit. You can argue with some of the things he has done since he's been there, but he wanted to win. He wanted to help that team. But now he sees it, he sees it's not going to work, and he's not in the frame of mind to play for them anymore."

This is what all great players talk about. They want to win. It's what drives us. Do you ever see Dan Marino's face when somebody says, "Oh, Dan, you never won a title." Shit, dude, his stare can cut you in half. People talk about how he wasn't the best quarterback of all time because he didn't win a title. I think that's bullshit. I grew up watching Marino and the Marks Brothers. Mark Clayton and Mark Duper were my heroes. Those dudes had style. They were exciting. But all these fans are on this kick of, "Oh, Marino didn't win this, he didn't win that." It's crap, but that's why winning drives us so much. It's like when you lose a game. You just want to keep playing. You don't care. You'll play as long as you have to until you win. I heard one player say one time, "When you lose, you want to play every day until you win again." It's even more than that to me. It's like, I don't even want to leave the field. Let's play again. Let's stay the hell out there until we win the damn game. That's what it feels like.

Look at Deion Sanders. Deion played for the money, he ain't going to lie to you. But after a few years in Atlanta, he got tired of that shit and said, "I'm out of here, I'm going to go win." He went to San Francisco and then Dallas and won back-to-back Super Bowls. Seriously, Deion got what was important to him *and* he got his money. People say he's the greatest cornerback in the game. They talk about how he shut down half the field all by himself. Do you think they would have said all that stuff if he'd played his whole career in Atlanta? Or do you think they would have said, "Oh, he was really good, but he never won shit"?

Now, let me just say about Deion, I hear he's the best that ever played, but I didn't see him until the end of his career, when he played in Baltimore. The other thing is, if I'd have played him in his prime, I'd kill him. In fact, let me call him right now while I'm writing this and talk to him about it.

Deion, what's up? I was just writing here in the book that I'd have killed you if we ever played against each other in your Prime Time.

Deion: I never would have allowed that. You wouldn't get a chance to talk to me like that. I'd just kind of keep you in your place and keep you quiet until you cried or something.

Me: Deion, I would have put a picture of you in my locker before the game with a check by it.

Deion: Oh, they would have had to change the time of that game. It would have to have been on a Monday night and they would have had to move the time up so everybody in the country could watch. Then I would have rushed at you right on the first play.

Me: Yeah, you would have tried to choke me. But you would have missed.

Deion: I would have got you, then I'd be done with you. See, I don't play against the wide receiver. I play against the quarterback. You don't really even exist.

Me: I like that. That's funny.

Deion: I do like what you did with the celebrations. You did a nice job picking up where I left off after all those years. You carried the torch, young man. The Tiger Woods one against us was good. But my favorite was Riverdance. Very nice. Gotta have a good dance. And the cheerleader one was solid. You played it up perfectly.

Me: Thanks, bro. But you know, I'm on punishment now. I'm stuck. I made my bed and now I gotta lay in it. Later.

I love that dude, he's sweet. Plus, he understands the whole game. People said he couldn't tackle, but that was bull. He could tackle, but he understood that wasn't the big deal. That wasn't what he needed to be doing if he was going to last, and that's not what a cornerback really needs to do. A cornerback has to cover. How many tackles does a cornerback make in a game? Two or three, maybe. Some cornerbacks are great tacklers, too. Nate Clements and Antoine Winfield are ridiculous tacklers because they're so aggressive. I ain't never seen anything like what they do. Champ Bailey can tackle, too. But if a cornerback can't cover, nobody gives a shit if he can tackle, because receivers are making one big play after another. It gets stupid if a cornerback can't cover. A cornerback is going to get all beat up if he tries to tackle all the time, stick his nose in that.

Same thing is true if I'm blocking all the time. I'm going to get my ass beat up and then I can't run and I can't make a big play. If I can't make a big play, then what good am I to the offense and how do I get the safety to back off against the running game? The safety ain't going to worry about shit if he doesn't have to think about me running over the top. If he doesn't have to worry about me, we can't run. It's pretty damn simple. That's why I don't block much. I'm a horrible blocker.

Anyway, Deion wanted me to go to Dallas before the 2008 season. That would have been ridiculous. Me and Terrell Owens on the same team? They would have to change all the games to pay-per-view. You can't just turn on the TV and watch that. You gotta pay to see that. That's like $15.95 easy, maybe even $29.95 per game. That would have been perfect on Planet Chad.

Speaking of T. O., that dude is way misunderstood. He's really a good dude. Doesn't swear at all. When he gets all pissed off and people think he's swearing at everybody, he's just yelling, "There's going to be smoke in the city." That's what T. O. is always screaming. It's pretty funny. But like with me, people think I'm all complicated. My life is simple. A lot of people think I'm flashy. In a sense I am. When I play, I'm having a good time, I'm extravagant, like I've said. But people who think I walk around in a big entourage, that ain't the case. Not at all. Yeah, I've got my boys I hang with a couple of times a year. But I'm not going around down with five or six people every day, having them hang on me. I've got a few friends, regular people, who come to my place and play video games with me, people I met when I first got here. That's really what I do. I spend time with my kids. I do some traveling when it comes to working, that's it. I've gone to Africa for Feed the Children. I've gone to London to watch soccer and hang with some of those guys over there. Other than that, I don't go anywhere. I don't travel. My traveling consists of when we play away games.

But I'm not against how lots of guys live their lives. As I said, I don't get into telling other people how to live. That ain't my thing. In fact, I couldn't care less what my teammates do as long as we're winning games. That's what it was like in 2005. We were 11–5 and nobody bitched about anything. We had some guys get arrested, but the fans didn't care. This last season, I was talking about that and stirred it up a little when I said: "You remember our '05 season, right? Our '05 season we were unbelievable. Our '05 season is the year everybody went to jail and got arrested. That year everybody got in trouble. So maybe the bad was a good thing. It sounds dumb to say, but look at it. We have cleaned house and nobody is getting in trouble anymore, no DUIs, no arrests. Now we're getting our ass whupped. Maybe, I don't know, maybe I should go out have a drink, get in trouble. Our '05 was one of the best years here in history. It was one of those years where there was a lot of distractions."

That quote got my coach, Marvin Lewis, all pissed off. He came down to me and said: "Why would you say some shit like that? To make people think there's something wrong with people." There's nothing wrong with me—I'm just saying, that's when we were good, when we were competitive. Big-time, we were the shit. With confidence, I was checking people off with my checklist. The whole defense, they created stupid turnovers that year. We would have two or three turnovers a game from the defense, picking shit off, making people fumble every week. We were playing great.

And see, nobody would be getting in trouble on Planet Chad. We wouldn't have to be worried about guys getting arrested or doing stupid shit. Not a big deal. Guys will mind their own business. In fact, there's not going to be any wars on Planet Chad. You know why? Because everybody will get their aggression out at the football game. It's going to be like therapy for people. All that stupid shit that starts wars, we'd get that all solved with football every Sunday in the fall. People would get so excited every Sunday watching the game that they'd be too tired during the week to fight.

That's why I should lead the world. If I was in charge, it'd all be cool.

I know what I said about being a drug dealer, which I'm probably going to get in trouble for. Then again, I said that shit when I was coming out of college and nobody seemed too concerned about it. We'll see. But I'm just being honest. Now, really, if I wasn't a football player, what I should have been is either a soccer player or a musician. My musical tastes are all over the place. It's like when people see my iPod and check out what's in it, I got everybody, every kind of music. I have rock 'n' roll, all these rappers, the Directors, all kinds of stuff. Old jazz, I mean really old jazz, like Benny Goodman. I've got Bon Jovi in there, everything. I'm all over the place. It's like when Maya's sister calls and we'll have something playing in the background, her sister will say, "What is Chad listening to now?"

Drive around with me in my Dodge Charger and it's all sweet. I was cranking up some Nirvana the other night. Bought the CD *Nevermind* and listened to that for a while. I actually knew most of the stuff on it already from Guitar Hero or Rock Band. Love that. During the week, when I get in early and pick the music, the other players are complaining. But I'll have Coach Bratkowski come up to me, look at me, and say, "How do you know about that?" Now, I mess with him and say the same thing back if I hear that he's listening to some old stuff, classical or whatever.

Hey, on Planet Chad, we're bringing Pavarotti back from the dead, baby. I'd have concerts every weekend. Oh man, my planet would be the shit. We'd have Lil' Wayne, everybody who is big now. I'll take the top five R&B artists, the top five rap artists, the top five country artists, and have the top five rock 'n' roll, of course. It would be an outrageous show. You know how much I love music? I paid for the Florida A&M marching band, which is awesome, to go to Cincinnati for a show.

So if I couldn't be an athlete, I'd be a musician. Could you imagine the concerts I would do? My show would be unreal. It would be Parliament Funkadelic times 10. I'd come down out of the sky, parachute out of a plane onto the stage while I'm playing guitar. The music would start as soon as I jump out of the plane, and I'm just going and going, grooving the whole way. I'd be in this wild outfit, all leather and all black, my favorite color, and the outfit would light up. Lights coming down the arms and legs, make me look like this big figure. It would be sweet. It would be off the wall. It would be like every Sunday when I touch the field, you don't know what to expect. That's how my shows would be, sold out, not even standing room available. "What the hell is he going to do? What is he going to come out in? What is he going to play?" You just never know. It would blow Prince away, anybody. My shows would be outrageous, totally over the top. Man, musicians have the life, awesome life, because your career is so long and you get to be so creative. If I could be any musician, I'd be Paul McCartney, without the divorce.

And I'd have some outrageous events. Dinners, parties, concerts would be unreal. I'd have my dream dinner party. I'd have Michael Jordan because he's probably the best to ever play basketball, maybe even any sport, and I would just want to know what made him the best at his craft. Everybody works hard, that's obvious. Like, I busted my ass, but what separated him from everybody else that made it? Then I'd have Donald Trump because he's so goddamn savvy with his money and he's so successful. Whatever he did, I would probably try to follow the same path, but with me not having anywhere near the financial success he's had. I want to know what he's thinking. The last one would have to be Obama now. That would be very impressive. Then, because I've had him over to dinner, he can take me off the goddamn tax bracket. But I'd want to pick his brain. I'm not sure what I'd ask him, but that would be a historic moment, Obama talking to Ocho. I probably wouldn't even know what the hell to say. I'd probably say, "You want to play one-on-one?"

That's who I should challenge, Obama in basketball. I'll give him five points. Can you imagine just jumping on the president and talking shit? I'd dunk on him and say, "Yeah, get the fuck up, huh?" That would be so funny, I can just picture it. Hey, don't cut him no slack, just rip him. That would be some funny shit. Although I might get my ass shot by his Secret Service, so I gotta think about this a little more.

But I definitely need to rap with Obama about politics. Not that he doesn't have a lot of shit that needs to get fixed. The economy is out of control, we're still in Iraq. There are so many freaking problems. I can tell you this, my man can have that job. But I can also tell you we have plenty more things we have to solve around the world. I know that firsthand from the Feed the Children project, when I got a chance to go to Africa.

Going to Africa was a really amazing experience for me. I did it in 2007 and it shocked me, opened my eyes. It was sad, and I don't think people understand anything close to what we're talking about. You see the ads on TV, you see the pictures of the kids, and you know they need help, but you don't understand how bad it really is until you go. You've got to see it. Being that it's so damn far away and people don't have the means to get out there, that's a hard thing to relate to. But it's bad, and until you get off that plane and see it and smell it, you have no idea. You think about some of the things we take for granted, like simple stuff, clean water, being able to feed yourself, being able to have clothes on your back, clean clothes, shoes, toothbrush, toothpaste, deodorant, just your normal basic stuff, it doesn't even matter. A homeless person in the States can feed himself. A person there who has somewhere to stay can't even do that. No bathroom, no nothing.

They call them slums, but this ain't like the slums that I grew up around. We're talking about people living in eight-by-eight or nine-by-nine little . . . I guess you call them huts. They're made out of mud and sticks, four or five people living in them. You can see them for miles, it's just all together. The bathroom is outside, it runs like little rivers throughout the entire little village, it smells horrible. Kids with no shoes, no clothing, hungry, it was sad.

I got to spend two weeks there with Feed the Children. We rescued a couple of babies. There were mothers who had just had kids, but they can't raise them or maybe the baby's mother died at birth, different situations. Mothers have kids and just abandon them, period, just leave them anywhere, wherever. I don't know how you solve it all, but we have to have a solution. Shit, we can go take over a whole goddamn country in Iraq, but we can't help people in Africa? If we wanted to wipe out the problem, the hunger, babies dying, we could wipe it out. We've got the means. I just think it's something that we don't want to do, where that's just not our focus. We can wipe it out easy. If you can feed a kid for five, ten, fifteen cents a day, do you think we can't wipe all that out with a snap of a finger? We spend billions of dollars to look for that damn Saddam and bin Laden.

On Planet Chad, we work this shit out, we solve these problems. We get people fed, we don't worry about shit like that, we get it solved. Hey, it's the way we do it. We get results and we have fun doing it. We're enjoying life all the time. Unfortunately, people don't get that idea. They get stuck in all the BS, all the politics. It's like how some fans and media don't get me. They don't understand what I'm trying to get at, how I'm trying to entertain.

I don't know why people don't get it. I've never understood why they don't get it, I don't feel like trying to prove anything to anyone. Either you get it or you don't. If you like what I do, then you get it. If you don't, then you don't get it. It's like that with anything. I don't see how you don't get it. Hey, let's score a touchdown, just hand the ball to the ref, and go back to the huddle. If everybody did that and everybody was the same, there would be no personality. Come on, it's got to be fun. I mean, what are you watching the game for? Where's the excitement? Having personalities, different players, different styles of players, that makes it interesting.

But people think it's just all about me and what I want. What I really want is that ring. I have all the stats I need. I got a shitload of stats, but I want that ring. When I finally get that ring, I'll probably strip right there on the field. Whatever it is, I'll be in the moment and people will probably make fun of me for it. I'll feel totally happy, totally naked, and that's how I'd want to be. It's like when I saw Kevin Garnett finally get that ring with Boston last year and the reaction he had. He had played 13 years, the first 12 with Minnesota, just going nowhere year after year. To be that great and to see your talent go to waste for so long. But then to get there finally, you could see the happiness on his face, the total joy. He was just screaming, not even really making sense sometimes. But he was saying, "Anything is possible."

That makes me think the same thing and just hope. Maybe anything really is possible. That was one of the best celebrations I've ever seen. I want that feeling. I really want that, because I've damn near forgotten what it feels like to win. I damn sure can't imagine that feeling right now.

I'll tell you this, it would be out of this world.